Richard A … Sense

Richard Asher Talking Sense

A COLLECTION OF PAPERS,
INCLUDING THE TRIAD 'SENSE AND SENSIBILITY',
'MYXOEDEMATOUS MADNESS', 'THE DANGERS
OF GOING TO BED', & 'MUNCHAUSEN'S SYNDROME'

EDITED BY
Sir Francis Avery Jones

WITH A FOREWORD BY
Lord Rosenheim

AND AN INTRODUCTORY APPRECIATION BY
Professor William Bean

Pitman Medical

First published 1972
Reprinted 1973 (twice), 1974, 1977

Pitman Medical Publishing Co Ltd
42 Camden Road, Tunbridge Wells,
Kent TN1 2QD

Associated Companies

UNITED KINGDOM
Pitman Publishing Ltd, London
Focal Press Ltd, London

USA
Pitman Publishing Corporation, California
Fearon Publishers Inc, California

AUSTRALIA
Pitman Publishing Pty Ltd, Melbourne

CANADA
Pitman Publishing, Toronto
Copp Clark Publishing, Toronto

EAST AFRICA
Sir Isaac Pitman and Sons Ltd, Nairobi

SOUTH AFRICA
Pitman Publishing Co SA (Pty) Ltd, Johannesburg

NEW ZEALAND
Pitman Publishing NZ Ltd, Wellington

ISBN: 0 272 00067 1

Cat. No. 21 0007 81

Reproduced and printed by photolithography
and bound in Great Britain at The Pitman Press, Bath, Avon

Contents

Foreword

By Lord Rosenheim

All who knew Richard Asher, who enjoyed his sparkling wit and were privileged to be his friends, will be delighted that his major writings have been brought together in this book. Those who read these lectures and articles for the first time will wish to know more about the man who could write so brilliantly and who so evidently combined clarity of thought and word with a deep understanding of everyday problems of medicine.

Richard Asher was born in 1912, was educated at Lancing and at the London Hospital, where he qualified in 1934 and held a number of posts including that of house physician to Dr Donald Hunter. In 1942 he was appointed physician to the Central Middlesex Hospital, where he became one of the team of young and enthusiastic doctors who helped to establish this erstwhile municipal hospital as a great medical centre with a worldwide reputation for its clinical work, teaching and research.

An excellent clinician and diagnostician, Richard Asher had a deep concern for and interest in all his patients. With his quick and enquiring mind, his highly trained powers of observation and his retentive memory, he noted the unusual in a patient's history or the unexpected on physical examination, and thus continually refined his understanding of disease.

When he voluntarily accepted charge of the Mental Observation Ward at the Central Middlesex Hospital, he further developed his interest in psychiatry and made his most important contribution to current medical thought by his appreciation of the many physical causes of mental disease. It was his work in this field that led him to define 'Myxoedematous Madness' and the 'Munchausen Syndrome'; diagnostic terms that have rapidly become part of our medical vocabulary.

At the height of his career, Richard Asher enjoyed a great reputation for he was not only an outstanding clinician, but a popular teacher and inspired lecturer. With his impish sense of humour, his company was never dull and his lectures were enlivened by many original and unexpected observations and illustrated by superb slides. His great interest in the exact meaning of words and in their use and misuse led to a precision and simplicity in his writing that will delight the readers of this book and should serve as an inspiration to future medical authors. He lectured widely in this country and abroad, was sometime President of the Clinical Section of the Royal Society of Medicine, Chairman of the Middlesex County Medical Society and a Councillor of the Medical Society of London. He was elected a Fellow of the Royal College of Physicians of London in 1952.

In 1964, with the increasing specialisation of medical practice, authority decreed that a psychiatrist should assume responsibility for the mental observation ward. Deeply affronted, Richard Asher resigned from the staff of the hospital and virtually retired from active medical practice. This action, which deeply distressed his many friends, probably resulted partly from ill health. Increasingly introspective and despondent, he nevertheless retained his great sense of humour and his powers of writing. He died in 1969 at the age of 57.

Married to a delightful and distinguished musician, his family, who have made their names in the musical and theatrical world, gave him great support and pleasure. His family life was a very happy one and, with his interest in people, he was an excellent host who delighted in good company.

Although a friend of mine for more than twenty-five years, I find it difficult to draw an adequate picture of this remarkable man. He was an eccentric in a world that was becoming increasingly uniform; he revelled in the clinical paradox and the unusual; delighted in poking fun at authority and pomposity; a modern Don Quixote.

It was impossible to be dull in the presence of his quick and agile mind. His great interest in his patients, his individualism, his sense of humour will be immediately apparent to all who are now able to enjoy his writings and relive his lectures.

London
June 1972

Richard Asher—an Appreciation

By William B. Bean, MD

Sir William Osler Professor of Medicine
University of Iowa

Fortunate indeed is any society if it can find even one person who sees and perceives clearly, judges exactly, and then speaks with reason and grace. But the requirements of the seer are hard. They are infinitely teasing, composed as they are of contradiction and paradox. Richard Asher, who would have said it much better, was such a man. We who cherished him with affection, now enjoy the legacy of his unique gifts. This small collection is but a sample of his many sparkling clinical essays whose elegant titles give promise of riches to come.

Soon after Hitler's war, I came within the gravitational pull of Richard Asher's enlarging orbit. The word had got around, and it became natural to look for his medical stories and essays with their unobtrusive brilliance and insight. I supposed that this formidable man must be some dark English knight on a crusade of his own, or a patriarch out of the Old Testament. Some time later, when I first met him at Central Middlesex Hospital in London, he seemed inconspicuous, almost to the point of invisibility, but seeing him with his patients I found that he cared deeply for them. This care brought them help and comfort, combining the compassion of the wise psychiatrist and the vigour of the scientific physician; but he was a nonconformist, and inevitably ran foul of the smallness of bureaucratic rigidity.

Soon, I helped Asher's friends and admirers in the States to arrange for him a triumphal procession to and through sundry medical schools and hospitals. One part of his tour brought him to stay at our home in Iowa City, where he alternated between making charming verse and playing sonatas, fugues, or symphonic pieces on the piano at any hour of the day or night. On his return trip he stopped over again, and moments after his arrival at the local motel he enlivened the gentry by plunging into the swimming pool, clad only in his undershorts, where he swam about with the utmost pleasure and unconcern.

Richard Asher steadily maintained a clear view of what was important and what must be done. Neither custom nor habits constrained him or kept him in thrall. He was convinced of the need for clarity and thought in writing. He was the illuminator of dark corners, some so obscure to us that we did not even know the corners were there. He wrote about what he saw, thought, and did with a precision and exactness that make his emulators despair. He had trained himself to see by following Wilfred Trotter's injunction to make one's attention incandescent at just the right moment. He thought with the exactness of Whitehead; and he spoke with the tongue of a master of English, attuned to the music of Sir Thomas Browne made current by the wisdom of Fowler and Ernest Gowers whom he followed in precept and example.

Developing such craft and skill as Asher's to the summit of artistry is not a matter of casual hours or of sylvan ease. The perfectionist wears out his own strength. He may try the patience of men with less clear vision or ears that hear no music. The search for nobility of sight, thought, and word has left behind a sad list of martyrs whose bodies could not contain their spirits. So, a sacrifice to his own high ideals and aspirations, Richard Asher departed from us, but he leaves for our bleakness and turmoil his warmth, compassion, clarity, and simplicity. When we read his words, we not only feel better, we *are* better.

I

*Clinical Sense**

It seems to me that clinical knowledge depends upon three processes—observing, recording and thinking. Each embodies a different use of the word 'sense'. Observing requires a sense of perception, that is skilled use of the senses: vision, sound, touch, smell and taste; this faculty can be called sensibility. Recording depends on the use of words in their correct sense, that is the art of making sense; here 'sense' connotes meaning. Thinking, I use here to describe the processes of consideration, rumination and deliberation which constitute clinical thought. Thinking of this kind requires the use of yet a third kind of sense; sense which is the opposite of nonsense, a sense of wisdom. These three kinds of sense—perceptual sense, word sense and common sense, this triad of meanings growing from the one word—'sense'—support the whole structure of clinical medicine. Let me put it another way. The whole art of medicine depends on the stimuli that enter the mind of the physician (or that structure corresponding to a mind in the surgeon), the processes that go on in that mind, and the material produced by that mind, as a result. These three things sustain the whole body of clinical medicine. The stimuli are the five senses of perception. The recording of those stimuli, and also their transmission, largely depend on the use of words. These words, according to their suitability for their purpose and the way in which they are handled, have a far greater influence on the progress of medicine than is generally recognised. Finally, the processes going on in the mind, the deliberations and rejections and ponderings,

* This and the two following essays originally comprised the Lettsomian Lectures delivered by Dr Richard Asher to the Medical Society of London on 9th, 11th and 16th February 1959. They were published in *The Lancet*, the *British Medical Journal*, and in the *Transactions* of the Medical Society of London (Vol. LXXV, 1958–1959). A much fuller version was reprinted under the title 'Sense and Sensibility', from which these essays have been adapted.

depend on sense: a sense of perspective, sense of reality, sense of logic, plain sense, common sense and even horse sense. Dare I include sense of humour as a necessity? No. I cannot do so, for it is not essential, but like a catalyst it vastly facilitates and enhances the process, and like a flavouring agent in a medicine, without being essential it gives taste to an otherwise unassimilable bolus of knowledge. The use of humour, like the use of catalysts or flavouring agents, must be restricted or it will interfere with what it should enhance.

The theme of this essay and the two that follow could be summarised thus:

1. Use your eyes
2. Use your tongue
3. Use your loaf

the whole being the concern of the five senses. Though I shall take them one by one I am well aware that they are rarely, if ever, used in that way. The clinician when he tries to find what evil is causing the illness, does not say I see some evil, I hear some evil, I feel some evil. They are not three distinct processes. They are not separate like those three well-known monkeys who, by covering appropriate parts of their bodies, arrived at the virtuous conclusion they desired. Seeing, hearing and feeling are carried out simultaneously, and supplemented by the use of the helpful but less informative senses of taste and smell. Yet, having mentioned those monkeys, I cannot resist pointing out to you (at the risk of giving you some offence) that the methods depicted by those statuettes are widely used by the majority of clinicians. We shut our eyes to observations which do not agree with the conclusions we wish to reach. We close our ears to bits of history which seem out of place, or to noises coming down our stethoscopes which are not included in the catalogue of official sounds we have been taught to recognise. We refrain from speaking about things that we observe when they are not listed in the official phenomena of the text-book description; apart from that we refrain from speaking our own opinions when they conflict too violently with generally accepted thought, or when they are greatly at variance with the opinions of those we fear. It is probably to our advantage that we do so, but it is of no advantage to the forward march of medical science.

But to return to our use of the sense organs.

We see the things we ought to see rather than the things that are there. We see what we expect, and unconsciously we dismiss the anomalous. The clinician is both blessed and cursed with this suppressive mechanism—blessed when he detects an expected and significant pattern, but cursed when significant irrelevancies are tidied away without being appreciated. The recognition of significant patterns depends on experience and education.

When the experienced clinician takes a history from a loquacious patient, he hardly hears the many irrelevancies and reminiscences; his suppressive mechanism turns a deaf ear to them and they are unconsciously dismissed as are the meaningless squiggles in the picture. Yet we have to beware of this suppressive faculty which, by producing selective deafness, selective blindness and other sense rejections, can so easily suppress the significant and the relevant. The patient with attacks of acute abdominal pain may not be heard while she is describing the chronic rheumatism in her legs, but that very symptom may be the most important clue to the origin of her abdominal pains, because her 'rheumatism', if it be enquired into, consists of acute lancinating pains like red-hot needles being repeatedly jabbed into her. When her lightning pains are appreciated it is easy to diagnose the abdominal pains as the gastric crises of tabes dorsalis. That is not an imaginary case, but a real one. Two laparotomy scars witness that. Suppression of sight can be no less important. Consider the appearance of the polymorphonuclear leucocytes. These are the conventional nuclear shapes we find in our text-books, but it was many years before anyone noticed their little drumstick-shaped appendages. They were there when we looked at blood films when we were students, but I do not think many of us noticed them, nor are they drawn in many of our haematological text-books. It was not till four years ago that Davidson and Robertson Smith pointed out that these drumsticks occur only in women, and thus discovered a method of distinguishing the blood of females from that of males which was so accurate that they correctly identified the sex in fifty consecutive blood films.

It appears that what we see, depends not so much on the acuity of our vision as on what we have been taught to recognise. Sir Francis Galton performed experiments with sailors to find out why they could see a mooring buoy at a distance where a landlubber failed to see it and showed that, despite their superior powers, the weather-beaten eyes of the sailor exhibited a far lower standard of visual acuity than was found in the man from the land. The visual stimuli reached the retina of the landsman more accurately than they did in the seaman, but did not register at the cortical level. The inexperienced man from the land saw but did not notice; he perceived without recognising.

Clinical acumen therefore does not vary directly with acuteness of the senses although such acuteness is an advantage. The medical student who misses an aortic diastolic murmur almost certainly has better hearing than the consultant who teaches him to recognise it. Clinical acumen depends on unconscious selection and unconscious rejection of sensory stimuli. In the plainer words of Polynesia, the parrot who belonged to that legendary clinician Dr Doolittle, it depends—upon being a good noticer.

There are two special kinds of noticing that occur in the highest degree in geniuses and in pioneers. The ability to notice the significance of what, at first sight, is irrelevant, and the ability to detect that which is common to several groups of data. An example of the first factor is Sir Alexander Fleming's enlightened scrutiny of a contaminating mould which had polluted one of his culture plates. Such apparent trivialities may fall on a million sense-organs before they blossom into interpretation.

There is a special word for this faculty—Serendipity, coined by Horace Wapole in 1784 and defined as 'the faculty of making happy and unexplained discoveries by accident'; but luck alone is not enough. You need to be a good noticer. As Jane Austen wrote in *Emma*: 'Depend upon it, a lucky guess is never merely luck, there is always some talent in it.'

This gift of seeing the gold that glitters among the dross may depend upon negative observations; it includes what you do not see as well as what you do see and what you do not hear as well as what you hear.

'May I call your attention to the singular incident of the dog in the night time', said Sherlock Holmes. 'But the dog did nothing in the night time', said Dr Watson. 'That', said Holmes, 'is the singular incident.'

In medicine there have been similar important negatives: in 1897 Sir James Mackenzie was examining an old patient of his with mitral stenosis who had suddenly developed extreme heart failure with a rapid irregular action of the heart. He saw that there was no auricular wave in the jugular veins and he heard that there was no presystolic murmur. In fact, he heard and saw nothing. The auricle was doing nothing, and that was the significant incident. That was how auricular fibrillation was discovered; though in that year he described it as paralysis of the auricle. To quote from his original writing, he said: 'For many years I speculated as to what the auricle was doing after it ceased to appear in the tracings; when Dr Lewis adduced experimental proof that cessation of auricular activity was due to fibrillation I had no hesitation in accepting the term.' Now we know that the circus movement of Sir Thomas Lewis does not really take place, Sir James Mackenzie does not seem to have been so wide off the mark with his term—paralysis. The absence of dental caries in fluoride-rich districts and the absence of smallpox among dairymaids are further examples of observation of negative type which have led to enormous clinical advances, though the absence of coronary disease among Bantus remains an unsolved mystery.

The second faculty of seeing what is common to otherwise dissimilar patterns is of incalculable value, not only in clinical medicine but also in passing the eleven plus, where a familiar type of question is: 'Which of these have something in common', followed by a diagram or a series of figures.

The first stage in a discovery of major clinical importance is often the observation, in a series of puzzling cases, that though they differ in many ways there is one factor common to all of them. Let me give you an example. The commonest cause of infantile blindness today is retro-lental fibroplasia and until a few years ago the incidence was steadily going up. It had been noticed that it occurred far more commonly in children who had been born prematurely: that was a factor, but not the highest common factor. The H.C.F., as we used to call it at school when we sought it in arithmetic problems, was that every one of the blind children had not only been a premature baby but had also been given oxygen. The detection of this common factor has prevented hundreds of children from going blind.

I cannot resist recounting to you another puzzling epidemic solved purely by good 'noticing'[1] and by the observation of a rather unusual common factor. In 1947 there was an epidemic of bullous erythema in Dundee. All cases were women and in all of them the lesions were situated in a band across the back of both calves at exactly the same height from the ground, whatever the size of the affected person. There were no marks on the stockings, so chemical burns were excluded. When the number of people involved had reached epidemic proportions, one particularly observant patient noticed that her attacks of blistering of the calf always came on a few hours after she had travelled on one particular tram route, and she also noticed that she recognised many of the other people affected in the epidemic as fellow travellers on this same route. A careful inspection of all the trams was made and it was found that one tram alone had been responsible for the entire outbreak. In this vehicle there was found to be a longitudinal groove at the bottom of the vertical slat of wood which held the leather seats in place. In this groove there was a large, well-established colony of bed bugs, at just the place where women's calves would touch the wood when they sat down and put their feet as far back as possible. It was clear that these bugs had reversed their normal mode of life, lying hidden at night when the tram was in the garage and by day sitting in a row feeding from the plentiful and constantly changing supply of calves presented to them. The tram was disinfected and the groove planed out to prevent its reoccupation by these undesirable tenants, and the epidemic came to an abrupt end.

The recognition of something common to several patients constitutes one kind of clinical sense. Anybody who has seen several Mongols or a number of cases of myxoedema soon notices that though individual cases differ widely in appearance there is something common to all, something very hard to put into words, but like a family likeness, a similarity which extends throughout a group of otherwise dissimilar people.

So far, I have discussed the clinical use of the senses generally: the selection of sense data, the exclusion of irrelevant stimuli, the recognition of the patterns built up by previous experience and by education, and the recognition of the highest common factor in a series of cases. I now pass to the individual use of the senses. Without doubt, sight takes first place. The number of important clinical data that can be seen is greater than any available to the other senses.

Colour. We can learn to recognise the plum colour of polycythaemia, the ruby colour of the alcoholic, the pale lemon colour of pernicious anaemia and the violet-grey of cyanosis. Moreover we may learn much from the colour of the urine: the rose colour of anthocyanuria, the iridescent pink of eosinuria (from eating coloured sweets), the opal pink of haematuria, and the peculiar green urine of people who are taking De Witt's kidney and bladder pills (which contain methylene blue).

Shape. We recognise the broad-shaped hand and spatulate fingers of acromegaly, the spidery witch-like hands of arachnodactyly (in Marfan's syndrome) and the distorted skull of the hydrocephalic child.

Movements. There are various gaits such as congenital disease of hip, Parkinson's disease, and the different ataxias from loss of position sense and loss of co-ordination. There are, also, the different involuntary movements of Sydenham's chorea and Huntington's chorea, and the different tremblings of Graves's disease, Parkinsonism and alcoholism. And apart from those there are other unnamed movements that enlighten the clinician: the restless plucking at the bed clothes called carphology, alleged to be typical of typhoid delirium, but in my experience more usual in senile dementia or in blindness; the restless head-turning and lip-smacking of the bleeding ulcer; and those movements made by patients while giving the history—the single pointing finger of the man with peptic ulcer pain; the circulating spread-out hand of the man with colic; and the sponge-squeezing hands approaching the sternum as they describe the pain in cardiac ischaemia. This movement is almost diagnostic of coronary disease. Dr Byron Evans first called my attention to it.

Position. The position of a patient in bed (the decubitus) may be highly informative, for example in myxoedema—huddling under a mound of bedclothes, or in a meningitis with head flung back. A far commoner decubitus is that found after a stroke, where the fact that one arm is under the bedclothes and the other outside, coupled with the well-known movement of the head away from the paralysed side, may reveal a diagnosis missed on routine examination; this position is often assumed even in quite mild hemiparesis.

Though nobody has dignified the sitting position with a name, the *deseditus*, as it could be called, is occasionally equally revealing. When a patient is giving a history her anxiety can be measured roughly by the distance of the sacrum from the back of the chair. As anxiety mounts, so does the distance increase until the patient is perched on the edge in imminent danger. I once impressed my houseman by solving a mysterious case of PUO purely by means of the *deseditus*. Ten days' high fever had followed a straightforward pneumonia, and yet the chest had cleared after penicillin. As I encountered this lady on my round I noticed she was sitting crookedly in her bed and I asked her why. 'I've got a pain here', she said, and she rolled over to display a large abscess of the buttock caused by a contaminated penicillin injection. This was obviously and literally the seat of the trouble.

While I am talking about posture and its use in diagnosis, I wish to describe a characteristic posture that occurs in one dreadful disease about which I have learned only recently. It is an old disease which everyone in this room has seen at some time or other, but, until Dr Russell Barton pointed out to me the characteristic posture occurring in this illness and told me his views about the causes and treatment of it, I had observed it without being properly aware of its significance. It is 'institutional neurosis'—the syndrome of submissiveness, isolation, loss of individuality, automaton-like rigidity, and loss of all initiative which occurs in people who have been in institutions for a long while. If it occurs in a mental hospital, it is almost invariably assumed to be an end result of mental illness. This is not so. This dreadful thing is caused by institutional life and nothing more. It is not confined to mental hospitals, but is found all over the world in orphanages, prisons, convents, homes for displaced persons, prisoner-of-war camps, and the chronic wards of municipal hospitals.

Because this disease has a characteristic posture which is recognisable at a glance, I include it in use of sight in diagnosis. If I say more about it than I do about other diseases which have characteristic postures, it is only because I think it is of tremendous importance and because I believe that you know far less about it than the other illnesses I mentioned.

People afflicted by this man-made disease have no resentment at what has been done to them; indeed, when the disease has got its grip on them they often resent efforts made to cure it. They are not interested in the future, they have developed a resigned acceptance that everything will go on as it is: inevitably, unchangingly, and indefinitely.

Characteristically, the hands are held across the body or tucked behind an apron; the shoulders drooped and the head held forward. Entries in the notes (if any are kept) give further confirmation of the diagnosis, thus: 'Dull, apathetic and childish', 'Mute, dirty and withdrawn', or alternatively, 'Has settled down well' or 'Is co-operative, and gives no trouble.'

From *posture* I pass to the expression, but I will refer only to its use in psychiatry, where, for instance, we may see the profound misery of melancholia, the infectious rapture of mania, the vacuous fatuity of G.P.I., and the eerie un-warming smile of schizophrenia.

I now turn to the use of hearing, the next in order of importance. I shall only consider the use of the naked ear. There is not time to consider what can be heard down stethoscopes, or other instruments.

The first important thing to be heard by the clinician is the voice of his patient. With myxoedema, the quality of the voice may be often more helpful than the history that voice relates. The speech is low, and thick and slow, with a croaking quality that is diagnostic.

Many other voices are clinically diagnostic, such as cleft palate, diphtheritic palatal palsy, and myasthenia gravis; the myasthenic voice shows weakness and increasing nasal intonation as speech tires the palatal muscles. The striking change after an injection of prostigmine is one of the most dramatic sound changes in medicine. Slurred speech classically occurs in G.P.I., but is rarely diagnostic because it may be caused also by drunkenness, a sore tongue or merely slovenly articulation. A particular kind of slurred, spastic speech, painfully crawling from one word to another is characteristic of disseminated sclerosis.

Apart from the voice; even a cough may be revealing. The short painful cough of lobar pneumonia. The cough of pertussis—a diminuendo trail of little coughs with an apnoeic climax and followed by the unmistakable unforgettable whoop. And commonest of all, the familiar sound of chronic bronchitis.

The sound of breathing itself does not always need a stethoscope to hear it. There is the expiratory sibilant wheeze of asthma, the jerky short breaths of pneumonia, the deep slow breathing of diabetic coma, and that strange unending repetitive cycle of Cheyne Stokes respiration. It is easily missed because each cycle takes so long that you have to stop still and listen. Snoring, *per se*, signifies little except sleep, moreover, though commonly believed to show deep sleep it frequently occurs during a light doze, such as may be taken during a long Lettsomian Lecture. But the onset of very loud snoring in a hitherto silent sleeper is a little-recognised symptom of myxoedema, and its disappearance after the administration of thryoid is gratifying not only to the patient (and to her husband), but serves to confirm the diagnosis.

On rare occasions, various noises originating from the chest and the heart can be heard at the bedside without any amplification.

William Bean[2] has collected some of the more striking examples of sounds heard at a distance from the chest. One patient with acute pericarditis complicated by pneumopericardium developed such a loud exo-cardial murmur that not only did it keep him awake, but it also kept his wife awake, and she had to sleep in another room. Another case of pneumopericardium that Bean reports had a more unusual cause (though the sound effects were just as loud). It arose after a careless performance by a professional sword swallower. Other patients who developed sudden noises in their chests were examples of ruptured aortic valve, a condition usually occurring when sudden exertion is performed by a man with an already diseased aortic valve. A man moving a piano downstairs suddenly felt something 'go' in his chest and immediately those around him remarked that there was a noise like that of a young frog. Another man while engaged in a drunken brawl was interrupted by a sudden cooing noise like that of the soft cooing doves. In this latter case again, the wife of the patient complained of the noise at night, despite its traditionally soothing quality. The most impressive example of ruptured aortic valve from the point of view of audibility was recounted to me at the lunch table by my friend Dr Keith Ball. His patient also felt something 'go' while he was lifting heavy castings at his work and his work-mates assisted him home with a sound of machinery coming from his praecordium, a sound so loud that as he was being assisted up the path his wife heard the noise of machinery through her front door, and came to see what was going on (wondering whether the new lawn mower had arrived).

These loud endogenous noises are not often of great diagnostic assistance, but Allen reported a lady with an obscure anaemia who developed a rhythmic splashing sound like that of a water mill. This led to the discovery of a large hiatus hernia, bleeding from which had caused her anaemia. The churning noises had been caused by the heart beating against the intra-thoracic stomach.

I became interested in the subject myself when I was convalescing from virus pneumonia which had been complicated by the physician aspirating my chest for non-existent pus; this gave me a moderate sized pneumothorax on top of the pneumonia. Five days later, when I was just beginning to get back my breath, I became conscious of a rather satisfying, not unpleasant, twanging sensation arising from my left chest and accompanied by a loud click which I seemed to hear quite easily, though I wondered whether I was really only feeling it. My first thought was that I needed witnesses of this otherwise tall story; to my delight, two of the doctors at the hospital dropped in to see me shortly afterwards and I made them stand at the foot of my bed and solemnly witness that they could hear my heart beating from the foot of the bed. The sound lasted for some two or three days, and I found its loudness was greatest when I held my breath at a particular point in the respiratory cycle about three-quarters of the way through inspiration and lay slightly tilted towards my right side. At first I thought that I was unique, but I soon learned from the literature that spontaneous pneumothorax is the commonest cause of cardiac noises being audible at a distance. I have not heard of iatrogenic pneumothorax being reported in this way, possibly because those iatroi who accidentally puncture the lung are not anxious to publish their deed. Moreover, the cases I have read about all had left-sided pneumothoraces whereas mine was on the right.

Another sound occurring with pneumothorax and easily heard without a stethoscope is the splashing noise of a hydropneumothorax; often the patient himself will comment on it because he perceives within his chest an internal turbulence as of rushing waters which he can feel as well as hear. One of my patients with a hydropneumothorax complained that when he cleaned his teeth he felt like a human launderette. In his case the vigorous lateral movement as he plied his Kolynos achieved the same effect as when the clinician attempts to elicit the sign by a vigorous lateral shaking of the patient. The most remarkable example of externally perceptible noises from a hydropneumothorax of which I have heard was told to me, when I was a student, by the late Dr Theodore Thompson. He recounted how he had a private patient who was a hunting man and who had suffered from a chronic hydropneumothorax for a number of years. He found it no inconvenience to him and he regularly hunted on three days a week during the season. The only untoward feature of this exercise was that whenever he jumped a hedge the rest of the hunt all thought he had landed in a ditch because of the tremendous rushing as of mighty waters which accompanied his descent on the other side. Soon after Dr Thompson had taught me these interesting facts about hydro-acoustics, one of the cases allotted to me as a student was believed by me to be suffering from a hydropneumothorax. I can still remember Sister Charrington watching me with mild astonishment as I seized the frail young man and shook him to and fro until he gasped. To my delight there came an unmistakable gurgling and splashing audible throughout the ward. As I was looking triumphantly round me, glorying in this diagnostic tour-de-force, the sister asked me quietly: 'Would you like me to take this bottle out of the bed, doctor? It's making rather a mess!'

Noises from the abdomen are often audible to the outsider, as everybody knows, but their importance is social rather than clinical. Except in the case of carcinoid tumours. It is the absence of borborygmi, rather than its presence, that carries any significant meaning, and a belly that is silent even to the enquiring stethoscope is likely to contain paralysed intestines. The most startling noise that ever comes from the abdomen is the cry of an unborn child. There are numerous cases reported in the literature where everybody present in the obstetric theatre has been startled to hear the distinct cry of the intra-uterine child. The sound is usually short and somewhat muffled, but Livy records that an infant of the Marrucini when yet unborn cried out in a loud voice from his mother's womb: 'Io triumphe', which can be roughly translated as Whoopee! This last case is not so well attested as the earlier examples to which I referred.

Noises from joints are so often, and so easily heard, that I feel they should be mentioned here, but in my experience they have remarkably little clinical value. A joint is capable of producing a great deal of noise and very little disability, whereas another joint may be extremely painful on movement and yet produce no sound. All the same, I believe noisy joints are more commonly the site of disease than are healthy ones, and that when this noise arises from a diseased joint it is far more likely to be the site of osteo-arthritis rather than rheumatoid arthritis. The sound made by the movement of a Charcot's joint is supposed to resemble that of crunching snow; in my experience it is the feel of this sound rather than the sound of it which is the characteristic thing. The feel is in the hands of the clinician manipulating the joint, just as the sound produced by walking on crunching snow is felt through the boots as well as heard in the ears.

As the use of percussion of the chest depends upon sound, and as it is performed without the use of artificial aids, it deserves to be considered here. I think there is no doubt that the chief value of percussion is that stony dullness is a reliable indication of the presence of fluid; fluid in the chest is one of the few conditions where careful examination of the chest may reveal more than the chest X-ray does. If there is no radiological evidence of fluid, but the percussion note is stony dull at a particular part of the chest, then it is well worth putting in a needle and aspirating for fluid. Though I have put percussion in this section where the use of hearing is being considered, there is almost as much justification for inserting it in the next section on the use of touch. Certainly in the case of stony dullness it can be as much felt in the finger as it can be heard in the ear, and much more in the finger that is struck than in the striking finger. Apart from stony dullness, I have difficulty in being at all sure of other grades of dullness. For example, if I find the right side of the chest gives a less resonant note than the left I would, if the history suggested right-sided pneumonia, consider there was an impaired percussion note on the right; whereas if the history suggested a left-sided pneumothorax, I would accept that the left-side was hyper-resonant. To me percussion gives information about the relative resonances of the two sides rather than absolute information about one spot. Moreover, I am aware that when one side is duller to percussion than the other, I am sometimes only observing that the pitch of the note is higher and that both sides give an equally loud or equally resonant note. I doubt whether many clinicians have skilled enough hearing to distinguish accurately alterations in pitch, in tone and in volume of sound, and even if they could be trained to do so I do not think great benefit would accrue because, except in the case of the stony dullness of fluid, there is so little constant relation between the change in percussion note and the change in the lungs beneath. On the vexed question of percussion of the heart, I was told as a student that if ever I found the area of cardiac dullness when percussing a heart then it would mean there was surely a pericardial effusion. I think that was very sound teaching.

Next, and of equal or greater importance than hearing, is touch and here I group all kinds of sensation detectable by the clinician's exploring hand. First, temperature. Although it is better to use a clinical thermometer than to place an old-fashioned hand on a fevered brow, yet quite often a clinician feeling the chest for expansion or palpating an abdomen for tenderness, is pulled up by the sudden feeling of abnormal warmth. The temperature may have been normal a few hours ago when the chart was filled in and so his detection of a hot skin may alert him to an important change in temperature which might otherwise have been missed. The feeling of extra heat over an acutely inflamed joint or a bone affected by Pagets is also of diagnostic power. The feel of the skin in certain rare conditions can be informative. In Cushing's syndrome the superficial layers of the skin can be pinched up separately from the rest, giving a sensation as of picking a fold of thin oilskin between the fingers. A grosser degree of skin levitation can be felt as well as seen in the rare familial Ehlers-Danlos syndrome. In scleroderma the opposite obtains and the skin feels adherent, inelastic and immobile. Alan Read, an ex-registrar of mine, pointed out to me how in facial scleroderma one can detect this when attempting a routine inspection of the conjunctiva for anaemia. The lower lid will not turn down as it should normally. In gross myxoedema the sensation of dryness, roughness and corpse-like coldness gives the observer an unforgettable impression as if he were touching a lizard. In subcutaneous emphysema the sensation of palpating small amounts of air beneath the skin is strange and unique, the crinkling flickering tingle imparted to the finger tips being both diagnostic and satisfying. The old physicians attached great importance to the feel of the pulse, perhaps exaggerating its importance, but the feel of a collapsing pulse remains a valuable diagnostic sign, though why it has been compared to the feel of a water hammer I am unable to think. Few clinicians have felt a water hammer and many do not know what a water hammer is. As one of the few physicians in London to possess their own private water hammer I admit I enjoy playing with it, but it is nothing like a ollapsing pulse.

By feeling vibrations the palpating hand can gain much information because certain sounds seem to be easier to feel than to hear. It appears that the deeper notes are generally palpable, whereas the higher notes are audible. I have noticed that vocal fremitus is sometimes decreased over consolidated lung although the resonance is increased; this obtains when there is rather high-pitched aegophony. Fluid in the pleura seems to damp down the palpable vibration we call vocal fremitus, although breath sounds and vocal resonance are far from constantly diminished. To expect breath sounds to be absent over pleural fluid is a mistake.

In the palpation of vibrations of vascular origin the palm of the hand provides invaluable information. The low diastolic murmur of mitral stenosis may be felt as a thrill more easily than it is heard as a murmur. Not only can the diastolic murmur be felt, but the slapping first sound may be felt so clearly in addition to the murmur that the observer feels almost as if he were hearing the whole cardiac cycle with his palm.

I have become curious about which part of the hand is most sensitive to thrills. I have conducted trials on many students and found it is remarkably constant. In every observer whom I have tested it has been sited at the junction of finger and palm, mostly on the palmar aspect of the metacarpal heads. Try moving your hand over a moderately faint thrill and I promise that you will find that is the area where you will feel it most easily.

With the grosser thrills there is no need for such finesse and any part of the body can feel it. In one unusual case, I first noticed a thrill in my right knee. I was interviewing a patient with chronic schizophrenia who had just told me that the BBC were persecuting her by continuously transmitting radio vibrations throughout her body. As I approached her bedside for more details, my knee touched the end of her bed, whereupon I immediately became sensitive of the most intense vibration emanating from her right leg which was touching the bed rail. She had multiple arteriovenous communications as a result of an accidental shot-gun wound several years previously. Her views about the BBC were both inaccurate and coincidental.

Apart from vascular thrills there is the fluid thrill. This is an invaluable sign of fluid in the abdomen and more reliable than shifting dullness, though I doubt the need for a third party to partition the abdomen with the side of the hand, except when watched by an examiner. Nothing else but fluid can mimic the short flickering vibration which greets the left hand about one third of a second after a light tap has been administered by the right. With hydroceles, too, the fluid vibration can be diagnostic; the feel is reminiscent of the water bombs most of us made in our childhood from balloons, or finger stalls inflated with water.

Continuing with the information that can be felt, we have the estimation of tone by manipulating the relaxed limb; the flaccid unresponsive tonelessness of a limb newly paralysed by a stroke may be the most informative available sign in a deeply unconscious patient, particularly because of the way when released from the observer's hold it drops with a dead-weight flop which is quite different from the more leisurely descent of its unparalysed counterpart. The detection of increased tone is more difficult. There is a difference between the feel of spastic hypertonus and wilful contraction, but it requires skill to distinguish it. As a student I was puzzled to find that with a normal patient (and even more so with a subnormal patient) when he is asked to let his leg go loose, and the examining hands gather the limb into position for the knee jerk, this is the signal for the onset of muscular contractions of titanic strength which hold the limb as straight as a rod until, with a mixture of persuasion and Judo, the clinician manipulates it into the position he wants. Why the ability to let the limb go loose at will should be denied to all except those of the highest intellectual attainments is unknown to me, but for overworked deans of medical schools I commend this observation as a possible screening test for selecting students.

Then there is the most valuable of all manual sensibilities, that obtained by palpation in the sense of feeling for swellings, an entirely different thing from palpation for vibrations, though called by the same name. Here we are using a combination of touch, sense of position, deep pressure and joint sense. We perceive not a constant sensation, but a change. We cannot palpate except with movement. The movements required for this kind of palpation, whether for axillary glands or for the detection of splenomegaly, are highly skilled and only developed by both experience and instruction. They are not amenable to description in the lecture room, so I do not attempt to discuss the art of palpation except to say two things about abdominal palpation.

First, the convention of leaving the genitalia covered by bedclothes is kind to the patient, but unhelpful to the clinician. Not only may primary testicular tumours be missed while their secondary aortic glands are felt, but the angle of the palpating hand is distorted by the heaped bedclothes. There is no elbow room. The difference if all the bedclothes are pushed right back (leaving only a sheet if necessary) is remarkable.

The second thing is that patients in a warm bed relax much better than when on an outpatient couch. I have noticed several times when I have admitted someone from outpatients that a few hours later I can feel much more than I did before, and that I can find lumps which I had previously missed.

With instrumental manipulation much informative sensation is felt in the hands. The 'give' of a needle as it enters a spinal theca or an antecubital vein, the satisfying snap of a dislocated shoulder returning to its place and the particular resistance imparted via the instrument when a urethral stricture is encountered.

To complete the list of information that can be felt, I suppose that judging weight ought to be included. Quite small differences of weight can be felt. As I have an old-fashioned plate camera I find this faculty useful in deciding which of my plate holders are loaded. But I can think of no clinical use for it, except that a carcinoma of the testis, so it is said, can be distinguished from a gumma because of its greater weight. I can only remember encountering one gumma of the testis and I cannot remember whether it felt light or heavy.

Lastly, we come to taste and smell. I remember about ten years ago seeing a baby with ascites of such milky whiteness, that some of the wondering doctors thought it was milk which had leaked from some breach in the alimentary tract. Others alleged it was chylous ascites secondary to blocking of the thoracic duct. Dr John Humphrey, our biochemist at that time, was called in to settle the problem. He looked thoughtfully at a specimen of the fluid for a few seconds, and then he gravely took a generous sip. Without a moment's hesitation he shook his head and said: 'That is not milk.' That is the only time I recollect the faculty of taste being of clinical use. But Matthew Dobson (who, we know, was a Fellow of this Society), wrote these words in 1776:

> '*Experiment V*
>
> After evaporating two quarts of urine to dryness by gentle heat, there remained a white cake, which was granulated and broke easily between the fingers. It smelled like brown sugar, neither could it from the taste be distinguished from sugar.'

That is the first time sugar was demonstrated in the urine of a diabetic, and the experiment provides a vivid example in the use of taste and smell in clinical science.

Now for the sense of smell. The range of olfactory stimuli is large, but the amount of clinical information they convey is relatively small. Alcoholic breath is easily recognised, but may be misleading in cases of unconsciousness because so often it is the associated head injury and not the alcohol which is the cause of the stupor. Acetone in the breath in diabetic coma and in children who have been vomiting is easily detected by those gifted individuals who can detect it easily. I am not able to smell it at all, and yet if somebody is taking off nail polish with acetone two rooms away, I am not in any doubt about the matter. On the subject of uraemic breath, Sir Eric Riches told me he does not believe that uraemia can be recognised by the smell of the breath, but that the smell of urine inseparable from many prostatic cases perpetuates this belief. After reflection, I am convinced by this view because a continent patient with terminal Bright's disease can have a grossly elevated blood urea without any uraemic smell about him whatever. I am not aware of any scientific work that has sought to identify the substances excreted in the breath of diabetics and uraemic coma, and to establish which, if any, can be smelled. Is the acetone-like smell of diabetic breath due to acetone or some other volatile ester? Is the ability to smell this substance transmitted genetically like the abilities of 'tasters' and 'non-tasters' which are so clearly distinguished by the use of phenyl thiocarbamide? If the breath of diabetic coma is bubbled through a liquid, will that liquid give a positive Rothera's test? I am bothered that so little is known about matters which possibly might be settled without much trouble. Yet other matters of less moment are thoroughly investigated; for instance it is well established that the urine of patients with the Lawrence-Moon-Biehdl syndrome not only has a melanophore-expanding action on frogs, but produces in the minnow (phoxinus laevis) a reddish discoloration around the bases of the fins.

Continuing with smell, the sickly faecal smell of melaena is almost diagnostic, but not of great importance; the same applies to the pungent smell of paraldehyde in the breath. It is alleged that there is a mouse-like odour in typhus fever, but I have not enough experience to know if this is so. It seems likely to me that as typhus thrives amid squalor, dirt and poverty, mice are likely to thrive in the same place as typhus, so the smell of mice may be due to mice making a smell.

It is a common delusion among paranoid or depressed psychotics that a fearful odour continuously emanates from their bodies. A foundryman once attended my outpatients complaining that one month previously a new and rare chemical had been tried in an experiment in improved steel production and that this chemical had somehow contaminated his blood so that the fumes of it were still coming out all over his body. As I sat listening to him, tactfully angling for evidence of other delusions, the students behind me started sniffing restlessly, and I became uncomfortably conscious of an unpleasant, garlic-like smell, which increased till the window had to be opened. His story was true in every particular. The chemical to which he had been exposed was tellurium, rarely used in the steel industry because of this distressing complication. If a minute amount of tellurium is absorbed, the body continues to excrete the noxious gas, dimethyl telluride, for many weeks afterwards. With that account of an occasion when the sense of smell saved a man from possible certification, I bring to a conclusion my account of the use of the five perceptual senses in clinical medicine. Along these five routes comes the raw material we fashion into clinical knowledge. We fashion it by means of the words we use in recording and describing it, and also by the thoughts, sensible or foolish, we devote to its contemplation.

REFERENCES

1. Kinnear, J. (1948) *Lancet*, 1, 55.
2. Bean, W. B. (1954) *Cincinnati J. Med.*, 35, 121

2

Making Sense

In 'Clinical Sense' I dealt with the use of the senses of perception. I spoke of sight, sound, touch, taste and smell and attempted to indicate the different kinds of clinical information they bring to us. I was there concerned with clinical reception, whereas here I am writing about clinical transmission. My subject is words and their meanings, particularly medical words. The difficulty of speaking about words is immense. As my theme is largely to show the inadequacy of language to transmit meaning accurately, my task is logically impossible; how can I show that an instrument is inaccurate by the use of that very instrument itself? Even great men have flinched at the task. Two thousand years ago Lao Tse, a Chinese philosopher, after pondering on the problem for a lifetime, came to this admirable, if discouraging, conclusion: 'He who knows does not speak. He who speaks does not know.'

When, preparing this essay, I met those noble words, I was tempted to give up. For I, who do not know, am I who speaks. And you, who may not speak . . . probably know.

This essay is about sense. The sense of words and the sense in which words are used. I hope to show that the meaning of words has a profound effect on the progress of medicine, that words unsuitable for their purpose damage the transmission of accurate meaning, that words, though they provide a vehicle by which thought can travel, seldom allow it to arrive intact at its destination.

It is pleasant to believe that the facts of medical science are there whether or not we name them; that the truth about clinical medicine exists quite independently of the names we bestow upon it. If that were so, our only responsibility would be to agree upon symbols or words for facts that already existed. That theoretical ideal is hardly ever fulfilled. A little patient thinking will soon convince the enquirer that it is not just a simple matter of finding words to fit the facts, but just as often of finding facts to fit the words. When christening a baby we wait for the child to be born and then we find a name for it. When christening a disease we sometimes wait for the name to be born and then we try to find a disease to suit it. With children we announce their names in the Birth columns of *The Times* and with diseases we announce their names in the original articles of the medical journals. The only difference is that children's names have to be registered. There is no such procedure with medical terms. There is no Medical Registrar-General of Terminological Births and Deaths. Only medical dictionaries and the international list of classified diseases. These do not include every living medical term, and they list many that have died or that ought to be painlessly put away. There is something about a name, particularly an eponymous term, which brings into being things which never seemed to be there before. In creation the word may come first: the opening sentence of the Gospel of Saint John is—'In the beginning was the word.'

Take, for example, Pel Ebstein fever. Every student and every doctor knows that cases of Hodgkin's disease may show a fever that is high for one week and low for the next week, and so on. Does this phenomenon really exist at all? If you collect the charts of 50 cases of Hodgkin's disease and compare them with the charts of 50 cases of disseminated malignant fever, do you really believe you could pick out even one or two cases because of the characteristic fever? I think it is very unlikely indeed. Yet if, by the vagaries of chance, one case of Hodgkin's did run such a temperature, the news would soon travel round—

> 'There's a good case of Hodgkin's disease in Galen Ward. You ought to have a look. It shows the typical Pel Ebstein fever very well.'

The chart might be copied for teaching purposes, or even put in a book. The mere description and the naming of a mythical fever leads inevitably to its occurrence in text-books. One popular text-book for nurses depicts particularly classical temperature charts, attributed to various fevers. I asked the author how many hospital notes she had combed before she found such beautiful examples.

'Oh, there was no trouble about that', she replied, 'I made them up out of my head.'

I wonder whether any examples of Pel Ebstein and other fevers in text-books have similar origins. It does not matter whether or not Pel Ebstein fever exists, my contention remains the same: the bestowal of a name upon a concept, whether real or imaginary, brings it into clinical existence.

Out of curiosity I looked up the original papers, and Dr Burrows kindly translated them for me.[1] Both describe patients with chronic relapsing fever and splenomegaly but there is nothing in either paper to suggest any of them had Hodgkin's disease. Both describe cases of undulant fever and Ebstein suggested the name chronic relapsing fever, but it was very probably one of abortus fever.

An important example of the creation of a thing beginning with the word is gall-stone colic. There is no such thing.[2] Colic is a pain continuously waxing and waning, like the colonic cramps of food poisoning. Gall-stone pain after its onset steadily climbs to an agonising peak without any fluctuation, and then passes off. But the label colic has been so firmly stuck on to this pain that the pain is expected to be colic, assumed to be colic, believed to be colic and finally bullied into being colic, so that a man with gall-stone pain will be described as having colicky pain however steady it may be.

Contrariwise, if something has no individual descriptive term it has far less chance of clinical acceptance or clinical recognition. A rose without a name may smell as sweet, but it has far less chance of being smelt. Supposing we take an unnamed fever and an unnamed pain to contrast with the examples I have given. In untreated pernicious anaemia there is often quite a high fever. Sixty per cent of cases with red cell counts under 1½ million show a fever over 101°F. This invariably settles to normal levels within a week of one adequate injection of B12. I make no assertion that this fever is of great importance. What I do assert is that had it been called the Addison-Castle fever or hypo-cyanocobalminic fever there is not a medical student in the land who would not have heard of it, many doctors would be afraid to diagnose pernicious anaemia without its presence, and the proportion of patients showing the fever would rise sharply once the name got into nurses' text-books (because if they did not show the fever they would have their thermometers put back in their mouths until they behaved themselves).

Now for a pain without a name.* Have any of you ever had, a very brief, sharp needle-like pain, near the apex of the heart: acutely localised to one point seemingly inside the chest wall, but feeling as if something was adherent to it. Breathing sharpens it, so there is often a disinclination to take a deep breath while it lasts. It comes out of the blue, it passes off in a few minutes, and although acute it is not at all distressing.

Enquiries among my friends showed that quite a lot of them occasionally had this pain, but, till they knew other people had it too, they did not mention it; especially because it has no official name, and also because it did not bother them.

I circulated various doctors I knew, and also circularised fifty recently elected Fellows of the College of Physicians—to see if it was reasonably common. It was . . . So if any of you happen to have it, you are not branding yourselves as either grievously neurotic or grossly hypochondriacal if you admit to having it.

[In the second of the Lettsomian lectures, on which this essay is based, with the permission of the President of the Medical Society of London, Dr Asher asked his audience of medical men whether any of them had encountered anything closely resembling this pain in either themselves or their friends, and if they had, to raise their hands. Over a third of the audience held up their hands.]

There seems no doubt that this condition exists, yet, because it has no name, it has no official clinical existence. We cannot discuss it or investigate it or write about it. Whether or not the condition should be named I am unable to say. Though the naming of diseases is not in any way restricted or supervised it ought not to be undertaken lightly. A fertile medical author can easily beget a large number of clinical progeny by describing and naming them, but some of his youngsters may turn out to be illegitimate, and with others there may be much doubt about their paternity if others claim to have begotten them years ago.

A special kind of disease-naming exists in the patent medicine and patent food industry, which depends largely upon the planned creation of non-existent diseases, such as Night Starvation, Hidden Hunger, Tired Blood, and so on. In this highly creative and imaginative work the importance of a good name cannot be exaggerated. One

* In a Foreword to 'Sense and Sensibility' the author explained that the pain had been described and named four years previously by Miller, A. J. and Texidor, T. A. (1955) in the *Journal of the American Medical Association*, and that it might in future be known as Texidor's Twinge.

weekly paper ran a competition for an advertisement introducing a new disease with a patent medicine to cure it. Here are a few extracts from one of the winning entries:

> 'Have you shoddy juvicles? Do you moil at night and wake prinkling, with a throbble? You are almost certainly suffering from GLOIDS. Waste no time. Write immediately in strict confidence for our free booklet prepared by a well-known Harley Street doctor. Mark envelope Dr X. GLOIDS. Dept KZ. All enquiries treated with strictest confidence.'

Although this may treat patent medicine disease as a joke, it is a serious matter. We do not know how many bowel neuroses are initiated by the relentless persuasion of the public mind into vain strivings after inner cleanliness.

I have only once named a disease and that was when I described Munchausen's syndrome. I discovered nothing about it, its origin is still shrouded in mystery; I only described something that most doctors knew already and gave it a name, a name which was far from satisfactory, though I have never been able to think of a better one. Yet the effect of naming it astounded me; a large amount of correspondence on the subject has continued in the medical press ever since, both here and abroad; articles and references are quoted and requoted, new names are added to make it more confusing, and new explanations offered for its occurrence (the allegation has been made that it is only caused by the National Health Service). Finally, a psychiatrist and a psychologist have been making a special study of it for over four years; they have a flying squad standing by for 24 hours a day ready to collect cases from anywhere in the country. They keep them in for months (to the great benefit of the community) and they ask them what different shaped ink splodges remind them of (with less definite benefit to the community).

There are many other syndromes that have no name; for instance there is also no name for an unexplained bout of fever and malaise lasting two or three days and commoner in children than in adults. The layman calls this 'flu', but the doctor who correctly prefers to reserve this term for the pandemic condition caused by an identifiable virus, is powerless when faced with this condition. PUO is properly reserved for more lengthy fevers, and the word 'chill' is offensively undignified, except in the case of royalty where with dignity a Royal personage can be confined to her bed with a feverish chill. In hospital, the consultant occasionally takes refuge by filling in the diagnosis as 'flu' and then putting inverted commas round it to show he is unhappy. In his own home, when one of his family gets it, he is worse off. He mutters vaguely: 'Take an aspirin or two and it'll clear up in a few days. It's nothing much. Just one of those things.'

If this does not satisfy his wife, he may be driven by sheer diagnostic bankruptcy of names to call in a hospital colleague in order to show his wife that another doctor cannot do any better either.

I now summarise my initial point, which I have illustrated at some length because I believe it to be of enormous importance. The words used in clinical medicine have a tremendous influence on the subject they describe or purport to describe. They perpetuate illnesses, syndromes and signs whose existence is doubtful, they deny recognition to others whose existence is beyond question and, moreover, they distort text-book descriptions to conform to the chosen word. Clearly it is worth pursuing the subject of words and their meanings a little further, because they play such a large part in our subject.

There is one property of words which has belonged to them since they were first used. They give a feeling of power to those who know them, power over the object or the person named. However uninformative the name of his illness may be a patient feels his foe is partly vanquished once he knows its name. We all know the conversation:

'I seem to have an inflamed tongue, doctor. Will you have a look at it?'

'Ah, yes. You've got glossitis.'

'Thank you doctor. It's all right now I know what it is.'

Ogden and Richards point out that because of the idea that knowing a name gives power over what is named, children often like to keep one of their names secret from their enemies; even adults keep their Christian names from being used except by their friends. Every country has its story of a name that has to be discovered before an evil can be dispelled or a foe vanquished. Probably the best known of these is the story of Rumplestiltskin, and, as many of you have not read your Grimm or your Andrew Lang for many years, I will summarise it for you.

A poor but beautiful miller's daughter got into the clutches of a certain dwarf when, having pretended she could spin straw into gold, she was put to the test. She was in despair until this little man came and did it for her. After this he proceeded to a kind of blackmail; first claiming her necklace, then her ring and, finally, extracting the promise that if she married he could claim her first-born child. Very soon the King, finding that she was not only very beautiful but also capable of producing unlimited gold by a most economical process, married her and, later, the first-born arrived. Despite her entreaties, the dwarf would not relinquish his claim. But, if within three days she could guess his name his power over her was lost. She managed to get hold of his name by a trick and so she kept her child. No wonder the dwarf was confident that she would never guess his name, for Rumplestiltskin was the kind of name unlikely to occur to a nicely brought up maiden; it means 'crinkly foreskin'.

Similar stories abound in international folk lore that show the same idea, that knowing the name of a thing gives power to him who knows it.

> 'What is this strange skin condition with red rings which expand from the centre in widening circles?'
> 'That', says the dermatologist, 'is erythema annulare centrifugum.'

He has spoken the words of power, and the dignity of the profession has been upheld. To the laity, words give a feeling of power against a mysterious foe, even words like 'congestion' and 'nervous exhaustion' and 'catarrh', which carry so little factual content.

Other words seem to have power against the patient. If you tell a woman she has rheumatism, she asks, fearfully and tentatively:

'But is it arthritis, doctor?'

The significance of words to our patients is a subject on which systematic research could gainfully be pursued. Arthritis appears to portend to a layman a protracted and ultimately crippling disease which will leave him deformed and helpless, whereas uncomplicated rheumatism betokens a few aspirins, a bottle of liniment, and back to work next week. However, the naming of illnesses more often gives comfort than despair. The name provides an illusion of clarity where there was mystery and gives illness a tangibility which makes it seem more likely to be overcome. This applies not only to the patient but also to the doctor. Only a penetrating mind, such as that of Matthew Arnold, sees through the emptiness of a name. These famous lines come from his poem called 'A Wish'—

'Nor bring to watch me cease to live
Some Doctor, full of phrase and fame
To shake his sapient head and give
The ill he can not cure—a name.'

I appear so far to have spoken disparagingly of medical terms as if to imply they only provide comforting illusions, or suitably opaque coverings for ignorance. That is far from the truth, but I believe it essential to be aware of the defects and limitations of the medical vocabulary before it can be successfully used. I propose now to go a little deeper into the meaning of words and, in order to do this, it is necessary to dabble cautiously in that elusive subject the meaning of meaning: this is a matter of enormous moment, and on this subject Ogden and Richards have written a monumental work, but, even with their book and Stuart Chase's *Tyranny of Words* to guide us, the whole ground seems so beset with indefinables and contradictions that few people dare venture upon it confidently. The only exception was Humpty Dumpty, whose views were admirably clear and confident:

> 'When I use a word', Humpty Dumpty said in a scornful tone, 'it means just what I choose it to mean, neither more nor less.' 'The question is', said Alice, 'if you can make a word do that.' 'The question is', said Humpty Dumpty, 'which is to be master, that's all.'

This Humpty Dumptyrian attitude is not enough for medical semantics. When we use a word it has to mean the same to us as it does to the person we are speaking to or the people we are writing for, or else our impressions are tarnished on the way and our thoughts not transmitted intact. Consider the meaning of meaning as it applies to some words in the medical vocabulary.

First, there is the etymological meaning, the literal translation. For example, take the word 'meconium', which means poppy.

Secondly, there is the implicational meaning, the notions either true or false upon which the etymological meaning is based. In this case the notions are that meconium causes drowsiness like that of poppy seeds, and also that the foetus in utero is kept asleep by this substance until the time of birth.

Thirdly, there is the referential meaning which may be absolute or nebulous. In this case, the referent is straightforward, i.e.

meconium is the black thick sterile material that lies within a baby's colon.

I chose meconium as a word to start with because there is little doubt about its meaning to-day. But this is a matter of luck. Had the word followed its original derivation it might have come to mean 'the opiates present in the foetal stools'. Then, when there was general agreement that the foetal stools contained no opiates, the word would have died. Had it taken another turn it would have meant 'that substance which keeps a foetus asleep in utero', and various theories as to its nature and composition might have arisen and rival arguments conducted on whether a foetus really does sleep in utero.

Take another word—micturition. Here there are two distinct meanings.

First, what scholars would call the correct meaning, the definition found when you look up the word in the *Oxford Dictionary*. This is: 'a morbid desire for, or frequency of urination.'

Secondly, the meaning fixed in the minds of ninety-nine out of a hundred medical men, which is 'the act of urination'.

Academically there is no doubt about it. Miction is the proper technical word for urination (from the Latin verb mingo, mingere, mixi, mictum). Micturio is a different word, bearing the suffix urio, common to desiderative verbs which all belong to the 4th declension and express urgent desire (see *Kennedy's Latin Primer*, para. 132), but does that matter much? As we all misuse the word, we understand each other perfectly. But to say miction would be shorter, it would be neater and, what is more, it would be proper. And to use the Biblical word would be even shorter, and even neater, but it would be *im*proper. The two points I am raising about misused words are these—

Firstly, how long has a word got to be used in a wrong sense to make it right (for instance, in using the word tawdry the most exacting scholar would not insist that the article so described should be genuinely sold by St Audrey, which is its derivational meaning, because the accepted meaning has been current for so long).

Secondly, is the meaning of a word that which the dictionary provides or that sense in which it is used? When the dignity of time has conferred respectability upon continued misuse, then everyone is quite happy. We use the word engine for the motor of our cars, unaware that its original meaning is wit. It is the transitional stage which gives us doubt and discomfort.

On the first point; once a word has been mishandled consistently, it is useless for scholars to try to preserve its correct meaning. Like a bolt screwed into the wrong socket, the misused word forces a place for itself and at the same time spoils the thread of the seating so that the correct fitting will no longer go in properly.

Though you may feel unhappy when you use the word micturate in the wrong sense, you must realise that it is too late for you to put it right. We have said lymph gland so long that the word 'node' is becoming a pedantic interloper. We use hemiplegia and hemiparesis so carelessly that their nice discrimination between complete paralysis and weakness can no longer be preserved. Once misused, a word is spoilt for ever, so the importance of keeping words undamaged by handling them carefully and never putting them in the wrong place is one that needs underlining.

A good example of an accurate word spoiled by misuse is 'aphasia' which properly signifies complete loss of word comprehension, whereas dysphasia signifies only partial loss. If you read in the notes that a patient is aphasic it gives you no idea whether his speech defect is gross or mild. It is about as foolish as calling all degrees of weakness 'complete paralysis'.

On the second point—which is the true meaning of a word—the dictionary definition, or the sense in which it is used? There is no answer to this question, because it depends on what you mean by the true meaning of a word. We are now getting into the deep and muddy waters surrounding the meaning of truth and the meaning of meaning, and approaching a realm of metaphysics and semantics in which I feel most unhappy. Yet I know that the importance of this realm is paramount and I must ask you to bear with me if I wade about uncertainly in the muddy waters of meaning for a little longer. If you could see the multiple corrections and deletions of my manuscript and the paper basket by my side overflowing with the records of my unsuccessful voyages which foundered in this scantily charted region, you would realise that I am not an experienced pilot.

I start by taking an apparently straightforward term—ruptured plantaris syndrome. Everyone knows what this means. We all know it means the collection of symptoms caused by rupture of the plantaris muscle. You all remember this thin sliver of muscle and tendon, lying among the other calf muscles, it was so easy to find in the dissecting room, and so obviously liable to traumatic rupture; it was slender, largely tendinous, likely to be involved in sudden movements and also exposed to external trauma. And, what is more, you all know the syndrome—the sudden calf pain, so sudden that the sufferer, if playing a ball game, believes he has been hit on the calf and, if street walking, looks round to catch the urchin who threw a stone at him. A few hours later the calf becomes black and blue and remains painfully swollen for weeks or even months. The name seems admirable too, does it not? No obscurity, no difficult words, no doubts.

But you are wrong. There is the most profound obscurity, there is the greatest difficulty, there are the most grievous doubts. An abominable semantic crime has been committed, a single term has been knowingly applied to two completely different things without making the slightest effort to determine if the one is equal to the other, or even related to the other. A pathological process and a collection of symptoms have been given the same name.

Supposing a man suggested the terms 'Tic douloreux' or 'trigeminal neuralgia' should be changed to 'The hypopineal syndrome' because he was sure symptoms were due to hypofunction of the pineal gland. You would say politely: 'Perhaps we ought to wait a bit. Are you quite sure that hypopinealism is the sole cause of this kind of face pain?'

Even if the man could produce a wealth of evidence to strengthen his contention, a philosophical clinician would say:

'Well, I suggest you define hypopinealism as the underfunctioning of the pineal gland whether or not it produces any symptoms and keep the term trigeminal neuralgia to describe a particular kind of facial pain, whatever the cause of that pain may be. Then, if you are right, the text-books can say "Trigeminal neuralgia is usually caused by hypopinealism", but if you are wrong and hypopinealism is found to cause no illness except hyperemesis gravidarum, our heritage of accepted medical terms remains unscathed.' But, says our imaginary pinealist, 'if that were shown to be so, would you then suggest that the term hyperemesis gravidarum be replaced by the term hypopinealic vomiting?'

'Heaven forbid!' replies the clinical philosopher. 'We are rarely perfectly certain of the cause of anything, so if we name things according to their supposed causes, whether they be conjectural or indubitable, so shall we have to change the name of the thing if it transpire to be not so caused. And, moreover, we should have to change the name of that cause, too, because, having been forced into an improper association with a group of symptoms to which it should never have been connected it would have become so inseparably attached to and corrupted by them that it would be permanently unsuitable to return to its proper place in the medical vocabulary. We do not call sciatica the lumbar disc syndrome despite our views on its cause, and that is why the words "sciatica" and "lumbar disc protrusion" are safe from defilement should other causes for sciatica be found or different effects of lumbar disc protrusion be discovered. St Paul said to the Thessalonians (and it applies to pinealists too): "Prove all things; hold fast to that which is good."

'And Socrates said in Cratylus: "He who first gave names and gave them according to his conception of the things which they signified; if his conception was erroneous, shall we not be deceived by him?"*'

Thus ends the indignant peroration of our imaginary clinical philosopher, as he finally disposes of the foolish pinealist.

But to return to the ruptured plantaris syndrome, from which this argument developed. I chose it because it well illustrates a fault in nomenclature which causes more trouble than any other of the semantic abuses committed by medical men. Because the name of a pathological process (rupture of the plantaris) has been placed upon a syndrome (sudden unexplained pain and bruising) we are in an impossible position. We do not know to which it applies—the pathology or the syndrome—and so unthinkingly and uncritically we are convinced without a shred of evidence that the one causes the other. It is immaterial to my argument whether or not rupture of the plantaris muscle does in fact cause these symptoms. Yet all the same you may be interested to learn that it almost certainly does not. I have searched the literature and found one[3] genuine case of ruptured plantaris muscle (note—I mean muscle, not syndrome). A young soldier complained of a painless lump in his calf which he noticed five months after being kicked on the calf. A sarcoma of the calf was suspected, the calf was explored and a ruptured plantaris muscle was found, curled up into a ball, which accounted for the lump. It was removed and the man had no more trouble.

I also found innumerable cases of the ruptured plantaris syndrome, but in none of them was there any evidence that the plantaris muscle

* Jowett's translation.

had ruptured. I was interested to learn, as I followed my researches into the literature of the eighties, that W. G. Grace suffered from this condition.

If I labour the point to the limits of your tolerance I apologise, but I am convinced it is of great importance. To name a thing by its supposed cause, whether or not that cause is the right one, is a very serious mistake. To label by conjecture, instead of by observed facts is never either necessary or profitable. I am quite happy with the word myxoedema (which means 'a jelly-like swelling') and do not wish to call it hypothyroidism even though I do agree that hypothyroidism is almost certainly its cause. The ramifications of causal names are unending—so important that I must say that again in important language: the semantic incompatibilities of teleological notation are formidable.

When I was a student, blood beneath the dura mater was not called subdural haematoma but pachymeningitis interna haemorrhagica. This convinced everyone that it was caused by inflammation and held up the discovery that head injuries caused subdural bleeding, and that operations could cure it. Take another example. We all see middle-aged women with restless, painful, arms, worse at night and worse after doing the washing. It is a common condition and nobody really knows what causes it. Yet according to the wide varieties of causes that are suspected, so is it given as many names: brachial neuritis, the costoclavicular syndrome, the scalenus anticus syndrome, cervical rib, the carpal tunnel. This is impossibly silly. If this condition had some reasonable name like 'nocturnal brachialgia' then we could profitably discuss whether it was caused by a neuritis or by costoclavicular compression or by compression of the median nerve in the carpal tunnel. But, for instance, to discuss whether the costoclavicular syndrome is caused by carpal tunnel compression makes no sense, anatomically or physically. However sure of a cause clinicians may be, a diagnostic label must be descriptive and not causal.

Apart from causal notation, other types of conjectural naming are equally troublesome. In haematology, cells are too often named by what is guessed about them instead of what they look like. I apologise for the words 'what they look like', no proper pathologist ever reports what anything looks like—he only reports what it is morphologically indistinguishable from. The term 'red cell' is a fine one. May it never change, whatever we may guess about what a red cell does. Other cells are less fortunate. Look at the red cells found in people with obstructive jaundice, sickle-celled anaemia and other conditions. Instead of the usual pale centre they have deeply stained centres and so possess alternate dark and light concentric zones. About 1936, a young pathologist called Barrett, who was a fellow student with me, became interested in them.

He very sensibly called them 'target cells' which describes them very well, and involves no conjecture about why they look like this or what properties they have. Someone else thought they looked like navels and called the abnormality 'umbonation' which, though more fanciful, is at least not conjectural.

Barrett, by some brilliant research, showed that these cells were unusually resistant to haemolysis, and that *in vivo* they were probably bowl-shaped, and also much thinner than normal. Before he had published his work, two Americans noticed these cells and likened them to Mexican hats: not from their appearance in stained films, but from their ideas of what they would look like if they could be seen alive.

'They do not look like Mexican hats' they contended, 'but we are sure they would, if we could see them as they really are.' Now because of their tough resistance to weak saline it is surmised that such cells can hold more water before they burst than any other red cell can do, and therefore that they must be very thin before they start drinking it up. So to-day, Barrett's sensible word target, is being replaced in laboratory reports, by the word 'leptocyte' (thin cell) because haematologists are not content to describe in English what they can see, but prefer to describe in Greek what they can't. I saw a laboratory report being sent off to a general practitioner the other day. I suppose the omniscient practitioner is supposed to reason thus—

'Ah yes, "leptocytosis". Thin-walled cells—he guesses they were thin. Because he believes they would hold a lot of water he thinks they would be shaped like bowls or Mexican hats—if he was only able to see what their shape was (which he can't). In other words, he saw a red dot in the centre of some of the cells—yes, that's all perfectly clear.'

Haematologists cannot be prevented from thinking, but they could separate their observations from their conjectures. They could report 'target cells present', and then go on to say what the significance of this might be. The role of a pathologist is not to be a seer. His role is to peer. Gazing into a microscope is different from gazing into a crystal. Yet haematological prophesy is rampant, particularly in obscure leukaemias. Controversy on whether the cells are myeloblasts, lymphoblasts, or monoblasts is unavoidable, because instead of describing what they look like, the haematologist inspects the artificially dyed, corpses of grossly abnormal, newly born, recently deceased white cells, smeared on a piece of glass, and then he prophesies what they might become if they were to grow up (which they can't). No wonder then that when some unidentified blood cell is found wandering at large unable to produce positive evidence of its identity, the naming of it provides a good deal of dispute and controversy among haematologists. Whether this is the origin of the term 'bloody minded' I am unable to say.

I now quote from the first article I ever wrote some fifteen years ago:[4]

> 'Imagine a child found wandering in the street is adopted by three priests who each christen him separately by the name of Tom, Dick, and Harry. One day they meet another three priests who have behaved in a similar fashion with another child whom they have christened Harry, Dick, and Tom. Now if those six priests try and have a discussion on the qualities of the two children—whether, for instance, Tom is cleverer than Harry—they are likely to become angry and to settle nothing; and they will probably go home and introduce new words such as protomocyte pseudodickoblast and megaharryophil.'

I do not wish to be carried away from the main course of my argument by floating too far down the blood stream, so may I remind you that we are considering the meaning of meaning and that haematological words provide food for thought on the variety of meanings etymological, descriptive, and conjectural which may be attached to them. Remember, the meaning of the word 'leptocyte' requires a considerable knowledge of Greek, toxophilism, omphalology, hydrostatics and hat design to appreciate it properly. Other medical terms remind one of the conversation between Alice and The White Knight in *Through the Looking Glass*. The *name* of this disease is Graves's disease. The name is sometimes *called* exophthalmic goitre. The *disease* is called hyperthyroidism; and the disease *is* thyrotoxicosis. Four names all used for the same condition. This is not only difficult for the student, but spoils words we need for another purpose. We need the term exophthalmic goitre to describe the not uncommon association of staring eyes, with goitre but without any thyrotoxicity. By the way, notice I said 'staring'—a very useful word which covers the lid retraction, the exophthalmos and the increased glitter from the moist eyeball which altogether make up staring. Most of you probably write exophthalmos when you mean staring. The idea that a long word is more accurate seems to be inborn. For example, I am sure you rarely use that accurate and short word: 'stroke'. No, you write down cerebral thrombosis, or cerebral haemorrhage or cerebral embolus according to your fancy although you have little idea how to tell one from the other and even at post mortem pathologists may be uncertain. Though there is this short word which covers all three you choose a long word which describes a guess. It is odd, I suppose it is the dislike of sharing words with the laity.

As a physician, I have been trying to direct your scrutiny to some of the motes that lie in our brother haematologists' eyes, but I must not deflect your attention from the beams that lie in the physicians' own eyes. Physicians indulge in conjectural names too, and cause a great deal of confusion in their subject as a result. Not only do they label something according to what they guess is going on inside, but they sometimes describe something they are equally sure is not going on inside. When a physician uses the words 'diminished air entry at the right base' he will admit freely that he doesn't believe any less air is entering the right base; he simply means that the breath sounds are fainter there. Yet, when we physicians are sure the lung is solid and that no air is entering it not one of us would use the words 'diminished air entry'. We might describe bronchial or tubular breathing or mention the dull percussion note or the aegophony, but we would never consider writing diminished air entry. This is not an idle statement. I took the trouble to circularise a number of my physician friends as well as the fifty most recently elected Fellows of the College resident in England. Of the 37 doctors who said they used the expression 'diminished air entry', 23 admitted that they never meant what they said, and 25 also stated that when they really believed less air was entering the lung they would never dream of saying 'diminished air entry'.

When we say L-ventricular failure, how sure are we that the left ventricle is failing? We are really using the word to describe a collection of symptoms without absolute certainty that failure of the L-ventricle causes them.

Supposing a room goes dark, we may rightly guess it means a power station failure but it would be rather stupid always to call darkness power station failure. Surely it is wiser to say what we mean. In this case we could have a word implying 'acute dyspnoea and frothy pink sputum'—rather than calling it left ventricular failure.

Now though I have singled out haematologists and physicians for criticism, I have no time to go round all the different specialties chiding each for their terms. Besides, what about the psychiatrists? I prefer to continue with the principles underlying the use of words in medical science.

I have mentioned modification of diseases to suit the words that are applied to them. I have considered derivational deviations, and spoken of the pitfalls of causal words and the use of words involving conjecture.

What other troubles arise from words? Consider that deceptive but convenient noun—the word 'mind'. Because it has been christened with a substantive it is easy to think of it as possessing substantival size or shape or substance, whereas it is really a convenient term used to embrace thinking, believing, remembering, fearing, loving, behaving, and all the hundred and one processes which compose it. The mind has no more existence than the sight, the hearing or the digestion; it is much more a process than a thing. But being named like a thing it is wrongly treated like a thing. Attempts are made to partition it as if it were as solid as a boarding house, and psychiatric architects erect jerry-built cubicles within it, into which they invite as lodgers those shady Middle European refugees—the Ego, the Super Ego and the Id.

Similar structural alterations are eagerly accorded by the laity, who regard the subconscious mind as a separate, but somewhat improper establishment contained within their mental maisonette, but only approachable by the back stairs through a locked door to which only hypnotists and psychoanalysts possess a key.

All those troubles might never have arisen if this deceptively concrete word had not been allocated to the issue of enigmatic abstractions we call the mind; it is too late now to dismantle the rickety mansions erected on this pseudo-concrete base.

Widely collective words of an abstract kind are dangerous. Sir John Wolfenden, addressing the English Society recently, remarked how often we hypostasise and attach a word to some vague notion and then suppose the thing exists. He gave as an example the expression 'juvenile delinquency', which embraces every kind of anti-social behaviour from stealing a few apples from an orchard to bludgeoning an old lady to death. Such a term, he pointed out, though a convenient shorthand, is deceiving; have all juvenile delinquents really anything in common between them? It is so easy to bequeath an all embracing word upon a wide variety of things and thus convince oneself that they all resemble each other closely. Are we not guilty of much the same thing if we use the word 'stress' to embrace all the thousand natural shocks that the flesh is heir to? The same word 'stress' is applied to the deliberate crushing or burning of a limb in experimental work on anaesthetised animals and also to cover the strain felt by a financier making money on the Stock Exchange. It seems plain that most of us would react very differently to having our legs crushed than to making money on the Stock Exhange. Not only has the word 'stress' been allowed to run wild, but its headstrong offspring, the adaptation syndrome, has been given equal freedom to roam anywhere and lay claim to any unexplained illness that comes its way.

Many words in the medical vocabulary are unnecessarily confusing. A technical term should clarify and not conceal meaning. 'Bleeders' are so called because they bleed such a lot if they are cut. How puzzling for the student that they have a normal bleeding time. If it were called 'the puncture oozing time' it would describe it far better. Jaundice transmitted by serum is never likely to be confused with that caused by giving serum from a different animal; the name 'homologous serum jaundice' is ridiculous and I learned from the questionnaire to which I referred earlier in this essay that 20 out of 29 doctors who use it admit they have little idea why they do so. Among ill chosen words, the dietary unit, the Calorie, is remarkable. Although one thousand times larger than the physicists calorie (which raises a ml of water one degree Centigrade), its name is exactly the same except that it is spelt with a capital C. I know perfectly well that at least half of you had no idea this was so. I say this with confidence because my questionnaire showed 25 out of 48 doctors think food and physics calories are identical. It is not your fault—it is the fault of the word. Until a few years ago I thought so too; then one day, in a thoughtful moment drinking a large hot cup of tea, I worked out that it was about 10°C hotter than I was and so if my tea cup held

100 ml I was gaining 1,000 calories per cup. In a flash I saw the reason why fat patients never lost weight on diets and planned the cold food cure for corpulence. To find the answer on page 1 of a schoolboy's elementary physics book was humiliating.

One could go on indefinitely showing the extraordinary confusion of our haphazard medical vocabulary. I can only mention a few examples. As we all know, there are two kinds of white cell—the lobed and the unlobed. How happy it would be if we could say so. We manage lobed all right, by saying 'polymorphonuclear', yet we don't say monomorphonuclear for the unlobed whites; not only do we remove the morph, but having done so don't know whether mononuclear covers all the unlobed cells (lymphocytes and monocytes) or whether it is another word for monocyte. This was another matter I enquired about in my circular. I found, as I expected, complete confusion. Twenty-four doctors thought mononuclear cells were monocytes, 22 doctors thought they were unlobed cells (lymphocytes or monocytes), and 4 didn't know what to think.

I am sure we are more influenced by the vagaries of our vocabulary than we like to think; sometimes unconsciously. You talk about nausea and rēēching when taking a history, but you never write it down. Why? Because you don't really know how to spell it! If you put r.e.t.c.h. then you suddenly think 'I've always called that rĕtch when I read it'. At that moment, the idea that you have a word pronounced rēēch if spoken and retch if you read it—seems so ridiculous that you put the whole matter out of your mind and avoid using the word at all, except when spoken.

There is one kind of verbal ambiguity that is so subtle many people are unaware of its influence. Take the sentence—'he feels cold' which can mean either 'I perceive cold when I touch him' or 'I believe that he is perceiving cold and is desiring warmth'. I do not think I am exaggerating when I say this ambiguity is responsible for many unnecessary deaths. It is much harder to distinguish different things when they have the same name. Failure to distinguish them is responsible for the use of warmth in the treatment of shock. This practice is foolish, ignorant and dangerous. It is the result of muddled thinking. 'He feels cold', say bystanders touching the flesh of a shocked man. 'Let us heat him as quickly as we can.' I now quote from Sir Heneage Ogilvie—[5]

'A certain doctor calls the use of warmth the treatment of a symptom, but a symptom is something complained of by the patient. The shocked patient does not complain of cold; he desires it. It helps him by cutting off blood from the surface vessels, to make enough available for the heart and brain. The shocked man spends his dying strength trying to throw off the blankets and shock-producing electric cradles heaped upon him by well-meaing but ignorant attendants.'

Yes, words are more important than you think. Two ambiguous monosyllables—'Feel', and 'cold' can murder a multitude.

Finally, if I am talking about words I must say something about style. I don't care a fig for school-room stuff on the difference between phrases and clauses or the distinction between metaphors, similes and hyperboles. But I do feel strongly about style. It is only a matter of putting down what you have to say in the neatest and most palatable form. And it cannot be done except by taking a lot of trouble.

Four months ago a doctor wrote an article about bed wetting in which he drew a distinction between better educated people who plan a small but successful family and those with lower standards who raise large mediocre families. This is the way he put it (but I have condensed it a good deal). 'The mobile families described as showing a loose-knit kinship network and shared conjugal roles accept occupational emancipation and its consequences on interpersonal relationships. They determine the number of their children by a critical assessment of their own emotional, social and economic potential, and they strive to create one or two competitively successful children rather than a gregarious egalitarian sibling group.'

Well I ask you? When you take your family on a holiday, do you say 'I am taking my gregarious egalitarian sibling group with me?' Did some of you play an excellent card game in your childhood called 'Happy Families'? Do you think you would have enjoyed it more, if it was called 'Euphoric Gregarious Egalitarian Sibling Groups'?

Long words and esoteric terms have no place in medical writings, except when they convey more than their shorter equivalents; if you say: 'the capillaries of John's skin are dilated by the exotoxin produced by a haemolytic streptococcus growing in his pharynx,' instead of 'John has scarlet fever,' though it is longer and less[6] euphonious it is scientifically reasonable because it conveys more information than the bald announcement of the exanthem.

The use of esoteric terms is also justified in concealing something hurtful from a patient as when we talk of neoplasm instead of cancer.

The late Mr Robert Milne used to say, 'I think this history should be taken *cum grano salis* because there is a possibility of *pendulum plumbi*.' When a doctor wishes to inform another that the patient confronting them is rather dull witted, a useful if anatomically dubious expression is 'This patient shows evidence of considerable cerebral stenosis'.

Though each specialty has its own jargon, I must before I close, warn you of a new kind of jargon, whose cottonwool coils are being wrapped closer around us every day, the jargon of officialdom and the jargon of committees.

In this malignant hypertrophy of language, nobody says anything, they 'state', or worse still they 'intimate that'. They never think, they 'are of the opinion that'; nobody finishes anything, it is 'duly completed'; nobody is paid, they 'receive financial remuneration on a 9½/11ths basis'; nobody ever looks ahead, they 'envisage a long-term policy'. This language is a waste of duplicating paper and a waste of time. Incompetence can hide behind its opacity and activity be smothered by its voluminous folds. May I warn you of this deadly and contagious miasma. May I personally intimate to you that after due consideration I am of the opinion that it should be an integral part of your basic policy to take due precautionary measures against this obnoxious prolixity.

Words are, and always will be, a hobby of mine. If I have done anything to convince you that words can either stifle or stimulate the march of science according to their choice or their use, I am well content. I have cited some very poor stuff to show you the deadliness of bad style. You need something better now. As Stevenson says: 'Bright is the ring of words when the right man rings them', so here are a few lines of good English to leave you with a pleasant sound in your ears. The right man who is ringing them is William Harvey:

> 'I tremble lest I have mankind at large for my enemies, so much doth wont and custom become a second nature. Doctrine, once sown, strikes deep its root, and respect for antiquity influences all men. Still, the die is cast, and my trust is in my love of truth, and the candour of cultivated minds.'

REFERENCES

1. Pel, P. K. (1885) *Berliner Klinsche Wochenschrift*, 1, 3.
   Ebstein, W. (1887) Ibid., 31, 565.
2. French, E. B. (1957) Unpublished paper read at Assn. of Phys'ns, Edinburgh.
3. Croce, E. J. and Carpenter, G. K. (1944) *J. Bone & Joint Surg.*, 26, 818.
4. Asher, R. (1943) *Lancet*, 1, 213.
5. *Brit. Med. J.*, August 7th, 1954.
6. Haldane, J. B. S. (1927) *Possible Worlds*, p. 227. London: Chatto & Windus

3

Talking Sense

Clinical knowledge is based on observing, recording and thinking. Observation depends on the senses of perception. Recording and transmission depend on the sense in which words are used. Thinking depends on the sense, or otherwise of the thinker, and produces either sense or nonsense as a result. We say 'He talked sense' meaning he spoke wisely. To say 'He had the good sense' to do this or that implies more than cleverness or knowledge; it means he had common sense, sense of perspective, and judgement. In fact he had wisdom.

Now wisdom depends largely on the power of reasoning—on thinking to some purpose. A vast amount of information is presented to the reasoning power of the brain, but all of it comes by two routes: either the subject's own sense-organs, or via the words of other men (either spoken or written). That is why I considered sense-organs and words in the first two essays.

The initial mental processes to which information is subjected are largely unconscious. It is cross-indexed, mentally digested and stored. As Sir Francis Galton wrote: 'When we attempt to trace the first steps in each operation of our minds, we are usually baulked by the difficulty of keeping watch without embarrassing the freedom of its action.' We all know that several days after facts have been absorbed they have sorted themselves out quite a lot. Even in one night, a good deal takes place; that is why we say of a problem: 'I'll sleep on it, and give you my opinion tomorrow.'

Galton spent many hours studying this process of unconscious mental digestion. He postulated what he called the 'ante-chamber' of the mind, where ideas lay just outside the range of consciousness, but could be summoned at will for an audience in the presence-chamber of full consciousness.

He found that most people who have to write or speak on a subject fill this ante-chamber with relevant ideas and leave them unobserved for a few days. He concluded: 'the mind frequently does good work without the slightest exertion, and a man returning to a subject after a pause is conscious that his ideas have settled.'

'But', he went on to say, 'although the brain is able to do very fair work, fluently, in an automatic manner, it is questionable if it is capable of working thoroughly and profoundly, without past or present effort.'

Well, I quite agree with that as far as my own mind is concerned, and it is a very inferior organ compared with that of Galton. If I analyse my own mental processes I have to use a less elevated simile than the ante-chamber and the audience chamber. I compare the place where my unconscious reasoning takes place to an oven, and my conscious processes to a rather harassed chef peering into it at frequent intervals to see if any dish worth while is likely to come out of it; moreover, an inferior chef, who uses processed peas and ready made cake-mixtures, and who knows that much that comes out of the oven is half-baked. That is all I will say about unconscious mental processes, because, by their very nature they are un-knowable.

Turning to conscious thought, especially as it applies to clinical thinking, the important thing is, that being conscious, it is amenable to self-scrutiny; its direction can be guided, and its activity, though subject to fluctuations independent of the will, can, by a great effort be deliberately increased. Putting it bluntly: sometimes you find yourself thinking, but at other times you can make yourself think.

The scrutiny of one's own clinical reasoning is an extremely beneficial process, but often it is very painful. It can be done, by putting your knowledge and beliefs into words, and pondering, not only on the ideas that you find, but on their exact meaning, and on the meaning of the words which compose them. This is a most salutary exercise. A variety of it was taught to me by the late Professor Panton, when I was a student at the London Hospital. He told me that if I wanted to get something really clear in my mind I should go home, and try and explain it to my landlady's daughter. His point was, that when perfect understanding has been achieved, it can always be expressed in very simple terms, and that the process of so reducing it is helpful. I believe this to be sound advice for medical students and likely to benefit landladies' daughters. It is also a salutary exercise for doctors of all ages, because when an idea is reduced to 'landlady's daughter' terms, its wisdom or its folly is far more openly apparent.

I will give two examples of this type of exercise. I was given a book to review some years ago, which contained this sentence: 'A significant fact about our personality is that—there is a subject-object relationship subsisting between the personality and other existing entities which gives the perceived objects their "otherness" with regard to the observer.'

Applying relentless simplification to this rather difficult sentence by stripping off the veil of words in which it had been wrapped, the exact meaning at last lay bared before me, and it was this—

'We know what is us, and what isn't.'

Although the thought itself was not entirely new to me, I found the process of simplification was beneficial as an intellectual exercise and, also, the end result was of great help in giving the book the review it deserved.

Here is another example of this method of clearing the mind by simplification, but applied to quite a different thing. Consider the tanned red cell agglutination test for thyroid antibodies. This is a new, and important laboratory test, positive in Hashimoto's disease; a condition in which the thyroid gland is large and hard and full of lymphocytes.

Because this test involves fairly complicated processes and depends on a logical sequence of thought, it is amenable to this kind of simplification. To understand it myself, I break it down into a series of childishly simple steps in this way—

Stage 1. Electricity can carry proteins. This is called electrophoresis, which means 'electrical carriage', but not the invalid variety. Globulins are proteins, and according to the distance they travel by electric carriage they are called α-, β- and γ-globulins. Electrophoresis is easily carried out to-day, because modern electrical carriages run on cheap blotting-paper instead of in expensive glass tubes. When we use electrophoresis in Hashimoto's disease we find the γ-globulins are very much increased. Now antibodies are all made of γ-globulin, so when the γ-globulins are increased, it is likely there are a lot of antibodies about.

Stage 2. From Stage 1, we know it is likely that there is some kind of antibody in the blood of people with Hashimoto's disease. Now, people with Hashimoto's disease often have myxoedema, and we know that myxoedema is due to lack of thyroid. So it is likely, if there are any antibodies present, that they are anti-thyroid substances; (made, of course, of γ-globulin). Let us put a suspension of thyroid gland with the plasma of a patient suffering from Hashimoto's disease, and see if the blood agglutinates the thyroid suspension. Yes it does, but it is rather hard to see how much agglutination has taken place, we must improve the technique somehow.

Stage 3. If we can stick the thyroid suspension on to the surface of red cells, then anything that agglutinated this thyroid suspension would clump the red cells together and that would be easier to see. Now, red cells treated with tannin are known to be sticky. They are called 'tanned red cells'. If these tanned cells are mixed with thyroid suspension they get coated with thyroid because of their stickiness. So, to perform this test, we prepare tanned red cells, coat them with thyroid, and then expose them to the blood of patients with Hashimoto's disease. We find that in most cases the red cells *are* clumped together, whereas if we do the test on normal people, no agglutination takes place.

I hope that explanation is reasonably correct; my idea was simply to demonstrate the method of thinking, rather than to explain the test, but if anybody feels clearer as a result of that explanation, I should be very pleased.

I chose that example because there seems such a logical chain of reasoning behind it. If the technique of reducing ideas to a simple form, and placing them in logical order, is carried out extensively, only a few of our clinical ideas would come through unscathed. Sir Clifford Albutt once wrote:

> 'Our path is cumbered with guesses, presumptions and conjectures. The untimely and sterile fruitage of minds which cannot bear to wait for the facts, and are ready to forget that the use of hypotheses lies, not in the display of ingenuity, but in the labour of verification.'

He wrote those words about hypertension, but they apply to many other subjects, and they are as true to-day as when he first wrote them. I take them as a kind of text on which to base some ideas about clinical thinking.

If we submit our own clinical beliefs and those of our text-books to a ruthless analysis of the evidence and the reasoning which underlie them—it is likely to benefit our clinical intellect, even though it may produce feelings of inadequacy and doubt within us.

Consider the ubiquitous stress factor, now accepted as the origin of many modern diseases—peptic ulcer, asthma and ulcerative colitis. I want to read you a particularly well written passage on this subject, from the pen of a distinguished physician—

> 'Peptic ulcer—one of the pestilent camp followers of civilisation—one of the penalties we pay for our boasted progress, seems to be more than keeping pace with our advancement, and to be attaching itself especially to certain forms of phases of civilisation. There is reason to believe that it is, if not of modern origin, at least of modern growth, and that modern habits and modern modes of life have something to do with its propagation. This is essentially a feverish and a fidgety age, in which an unappeasable restlessness pervades all ranks and classes. The struggle for existence has become a mêlée, and the recommendation to "commune with your own heart in your chamber, and be still" is looked upon as an obsolete adage. The result of all this ceaseless agitation and ambitious striving, is that the gastric mucosa often gives way under the strain imposed on it. By a hideous kind of poetical justice, peptic ulcer has become a distorted reflection of the follies of the age. It is the miserable "otium cum dignitate" of the man of business.'

May I now admit to you, with apologies, which are not very sincere, that I have been guilty of a trick. I deliberately altered two words in that pasage. Wherever it said G.P.I., I substituted the term peptic ulcer, and where it mentioned the nervous system, I wrote in the words gastric mucosa. Apart from that, those are the actual words spoken by Dr Crichton Browne in 1871 when speaking on the cause of G.P.I., at the 7th meeting of the Medico-Psychological Association. It makes you think, doesn't it? We hold such very different views about the cause of G.P.I. to-day. It can still provide Otium for business men, but with—oh how much less dignitate.

In the case of psychosomatic disease, are we not reasoning as follows: The pace of modern life is going up, therefore because the incidence of peptic ulcer is also going up the pace of modern life is the cause of peptic ulcer. What price, guesses, presumptions and conjectures?

One might just as well argue that the use of wrist watches was becoming increasingly common compared with Victorian times, and that therefore the increasing incidence of peptic ulcer was attributable to the wearing of wrist watches. Among the guesses, presumptions and conjectures is the assumption that the speed of civilisation always involves stress and strain. Crossing the Pacific in a Comet is less strain than crossing it in a coracle, and cave-men were probably as troubled by shortages of suitable flints as much as modern man is troubled by his income tax.

The danger of psychosomatic explanations for unexplained diseases is that it is so easy to find them and they provide such a comforting illusion that something has been explained, when it has not. That is why I regard Crichton Browne's remarks on G.P.I., as a warning of the greatest importance.

It is important to realise that ideas are much easier to believe if they are comforting, and that many clinical notions are accepted because they are comforting rather than because there is any evidence to support them.

Just as we swallow food because we like it not because of its nutritional content, so do we swallow ideas bcause we like them and not because of their rational content.

Crawshay-Williams's penetrating philosophical study of irrational thought called 'The Comforts of Unreason' is a work I have found most enlightening, and its list of what he calls 'Comfortable Concepts' is most informative. One comfortable concept, that most of us accept without being aware of it, was heartlessly exposed by Dr Ronald Bodley Scott in a Lettsomian Lecture. 'The art of therapeutics', he said, 'is founded on the touchingly naïve assumption that there is an answer to every question it poses.' How uncomfortably true that is, and how few people have the courage to say it.

We always say 'What is the treatment of this disease?' rather than 'Is there a treatment for this disease?' Even the expression 'effective treatment' is a quaint one. We do not talk of 'mobile motor-cars', we assume that they move, because that is their purpose and function. Logically we should not give treatment unless it is effective.

Deriving from this I obtain an uncomfortable concept which I believe to be true, but which I find too depressing to accept. This is it . . . 'It is better to believe in therapeutic nonsense, than openly to admit therapeutic bankruptcy.' Better, in the sense that a little credulity makes us better doctors, though worse research workers.

I find this one of the most uncomfortable concepts that logical reasoning leads me to. If you admit to yourself that the treatment you are giving is frankly inactive, you will inspire little confidence in your patients unless you happen to be a remarkably gifted actor, and the results of your treatment will be negligible. But if you can believe fervently in your treatment, even though controlled tests show that it is quite useless, then your results are much better, your patients are much better, and your income is much better, too. I believe this accounts for the remarkable success of some of the less gifted, but more credulous members of our profession, and also for the violent dislike of statistics and controlled tests which fashionable and successful doctors are accustomed to display. It is an almost insoluble problem, and the majority of worth-while doctors are driven to a compromise, in which they muster enough genuine belief in their treatment to keep their patients happy and maintain their own self respect, while preserving enough doubt to admit their inadequacy during transient bouts of uncomfortable honesty.

I have wondered at times, what is the point of controlled tests which only reveal therapeutic poverty; yet to avoid discovering the truth because you do not think you will like it, seems too pusillanimous to be contemplated. It can all be summed up into 'Where ignorance is bliss, 'tis folly to be wise.' Here are some examples—

There is quite a large body of evidence to suggest that neither insulin nor E.C.T. affect the course of schizophrenia, but if this evidence is accepted, the implication follows that there is no treatment for schizophrenia except to keep the patient out of harm's way and to hope for the best. If this was openly admitted, the distress it would cause to thousands of patients and to their relatives is too sad to contemplate. Let us consider less serious diseases. Is there any pharmacological substance known which has any effect on the course of acne vulgaris or of chilblains? One that would give significantly better results than its inert counterpart in a double-blind controlled test? Are the many remedies we prescribe for these conditions better than nothing, or exactly the same as nothing? If we accept that in many conditions the effect of our treatment is unrelated to its pharmacological content, would it be more honest, and much more economical to prescribe a cheap, inert but harmless substance? We are certainly not encouraged to do so; indeed the whole of our National Formulary contains no official, intentionally inert preparation. No Tab. Dulcis Fanny-Adamis Co. No Mist. Oculi Mei cum Betty-Martini; and what an outcry there would be if there were.

So let us face the fact that until we have effective treatments for every complaint we must cherish our delusions of therapeutic omnipotence, even though Dr Bodley Scott may call us touchingly naïve. But let us at least have brief moments of uncomfortable discernment, so that we can separate those treatments which depend on faith from those which depend on pharmacy. We must keep enough faith in our treatment to make ourselves and our patients happy, while yet enough doubt to make the need for better treatment apparent.

It is also important to examine the illogical thinking in which we indulge on our road to a comfortable concept. For instance: Vitamin B deficiency causes soreness of the tongue, therefore people suffering from soreness of the tongue are likely to be benefited by Vitamin B.

That standard of logic is happily swallowed by medical men, to the great benefit of the drug houses. You might just as well say that rat poison causes abdominal pain and vomiting, therefore people who are suffering from abdominal pain and vomiting are likely to benefit from antidotes to rat poison.

The laity are equally prone to adopt comfortable concepts. One of the most irrational and comforting delusions held by the layman is the notion that his body is really a kind of motor-car. 'I feel much better now you've given me a thorough overhaul' is a remark I have heard on many occasions. Doctors are often guilty of nourishing this delusion when they make remarks such as 'I think I'd better check up on your heart' or 'You'd better come in for a complete check-up.'

Behind all this, lies the delusion that the physician is likely to remedy defects as he finds them; applying a little oil here, fitting a replacement there and possibly clearing out a blocked pipe. The analogy with motor-car engines is false, and the only point where it applies is that when the trouble is very serious the patient is very likely to be returned back to his Maker.

It has been held by some teachers that rational thinking in medicine would be improved if doctors were taught logic. I rather doubt this. Most of our ideas are accepted because they are convenient or likely, and not because of logical reasoning. Even pure research is seldom carried out in this way, and a good deal of the reasoning is put in after the discovery has been made. Sir Charles Dodds once compared research with the progress of a man, stumbling across a dark room, trying to find the light switch and upsetting the furniture as he goes. Once he has found the switch and the light is on, he goes back and puts all the furniture tidy again.

Formal logic is based largely on statements of the kind: All *X* is *Y*. All *Y* is *Z*. Therefore all *X* is *Z*. For instance: All men are mortal. Socrates is a man. Therefore Socrates is mortal. Medical facts are rarely suitable for this discipline. They are more of this kind—

Some *X* is *Y*, but I'm not really sure of it. Possibly all *Y* may be *Z* (as Smith has claimed to show) but Brown affirms that no *Y* is ever the slightest *Z*, and Robinson too has strong views, but I find them hard to understand because he uses *X* to mean both *Y* or *Z*, and he calls *Y* what I call *X*.

All the same, a knowledge of elementary logic might make us more critical of the reasons we have for holding the opinions that we do. For example, consider that condition called iron deficiency anaemia.

It is well known what type of anaemia develops from indequate iron intake (especially if there is an increased demand for iron at the time). We recognise it from the small, pale cells which show more variation in size than is normal, and we treat it confidently with oral or parenteral iron and the haemoglobin usually rises. But unconsciously we are arguing thus: Iron lack is known to produce a hypochromic, microcytic anaemia. This woman has a hypochromic, microcytic anaemia, therefore she has iron deficiency. It would be almost equally rational to say: This woman is weak. Addison's disease produces weakness, therefore we must treat her for Addison's disease. I do not deny that most cases of hypochromic microcytic anaemia are caused by lack of iron, but I criticise the term 'iron deficiency anaemia' to describe the appearance of the film. First, because the logical justification for this term is inadequate, and secondly because it involves naming by supposed cause and not by observed fact. Concern over such teleological notation is a bee, which has buzzed forth from my bonnet more than once during these essays. Thirdly, the description contains an implicit assumption of great importance which I will now discuss. It assumes that this anaemia is an illness; that something is wrong, and that it needs putting right. This assumption may be true, but we ought to be aware of it.

We could make two quite different statements, one with this assumption, and one without.

A. With. Iron deficiency anaemia is very common in pregnant women, more than half of whom show Hb levels under 70 per cent, which respond well to iron therapy.

B. Without. During pregnancy, the normal Hb level falls below 70 per cent in more than half the cases. This physiological change is prevented from taking place if there is an excess of iron in the diet.

I am not suggesting that either of the statements I have just made, is true. I am only anxious to demonstrate how an observation can be interpreted in entirely different ways, according to whether you assume the condition is an illness or not. Also, how easy it is to make such an assumption without realising it. You cannot say what things are abnormal, till you have agreed on what is normal. You cannot describe disease without describing ease first. This cardinal principle is often forgotten, especially as it applies to the word constipation.

Here we have all the elements of confusion. First are we naming the state of the bowels or the symptoms we attribute to that state? Secondly, are we naming an abnormality, or making a neutral statement about a function? If a man's bowels are usually open on alternate days and he comes into hospital 36 hours after they were last open, do we correctly write in the notes 'constipated for 36 hours', or does this not differ in meaning from the statement 'bowels last open 36 hours ago'. It is too easy to assume that the frequency or regularity of normal bowel action has been decreed by some natural law. We never lay down a statutory number of times that the bladder should be emptied each day. Why not? Why do we do so with the bowels? What is constipation. I looked the word up in my dictionary and it said 'costiveness'. Then I looked up the word costive and it said 'constipated'. So I cannot answer the question, or the many others I raised in connection with it. I can only reiterate Sir Clifford Albutt's words: 'Our path is cumbered with guesses, presumptions and conjectures.'

I have discoursed enough on methods of reasoning, the ethics of credulity and the nature of disease. I would like to have pursued a discussion on the meaning of the word cause, but I am sure you have had enough of philosophical and abstract matters, and so have I. So I turn with relief to the more solid ground of common sense or horse sense.

It is hard to define, and best explained by example. The late Mr Russell Howard possessed it to a remarkable degree and he taught it too. When I listened to his teaching I was always reminded of W. S. Gilbert's lines—

'On fire that glows with heat intense
I turn the hose of common sense
And out it goes, at small expense.'

One definition of common sense I would give is that common sense is the capacity to see the obvious even amid confusion, and to do the obviously right thing rather than working to rule, or by dead reckoning.

When I was a student, I was skating on the lake in the grounds of Earls Colne Priory, when a lady fell and broke her leg. There was much commotion and everyone was anxious to help. Many of the bystanders were acquainted with the rules of first aid and knew just what to do. 'Keep her warm' and 'Do not move her till the doctor comes' were the two chief principles on which everyone agreed. Maids hurried out from the house with hot drinks, hot-water bottles, and luxurious furs. Nutria lay upon beaver, and musquash was piled on mink. I skated gently round the stricken lady who groaned beneath her expensive load. The doctor seemed to be hours coming, so more hot-water bottles were added. Suddenly a very simple matter of elementary physics began to be apparent: warmth melts ice. There were ominous cracking sounds—first aid principles were forgotten, common sense was remembered, and we got her off the ice just in time. A few seconds and that lady, together with a very valuable collection of furs would have been lost.

Here is another story relating to common sense. Many years ago, I saw a fundus oculi with patches of black pigment on it scattered all over the field, so I asked an ophthalmic consultant go give me his opinion. He wrote in the notes: This is retinitis pigmentosa. It might be part of the Laurence Moon Biedl syndrome. Is there any evidence of polydactyly? Surely, to refer a man back to a physician to have the number of his fingers counted argues a degree of specialisation which has altogether obliterated common sense.

The well-known jibe that specialisation implies knowing more and more about less and less is not without foundation. When single-mindedness of purpose ousts all other kinds of purpose from the brain, common sense is lost at the same time, and nonsense reigns.

Here is what I consider nonsense:

Two years ago a man was referred to me by a consultant with a letter from which this is an extract: 'Investigation has revealed the picture of an Inadequate Psychopath with strong evidence of repressed homosexual trends. He importuned frequently to have treatment for his symptoms. Therapeutically he was regarded as a hopeless case. He was bursting with resentment, and his conduct subsequent to treatment showed he was of a paranoid and litigious frame of mind.'

I made an appointment for him rather reluctantly. He sounded a particularly unattractive fellow. Then he came to my out-patients. He was a pleasant, co-operative happily married engineering draughtsman. He had never felt a homosexual desire in his life. He was suffering from severe pruritus ani and was extremely anxious to get rid of it. On no more evidence than an itching anus, the consultant interpreted his symptoms as showing repressed homosexuality and when the man asked for treatment, that was considered even more abnormal—he was regarded as importuning. The patient's practitioner was given a letter to this effect which he showed to the patient. To be stamped as a homosexual psychopath importuning for unnatural practices solely because his anus tickled was enough to annoy this man, but even his righteous indignation was interpreted as proof that he was of a paranoid and litigious nature. I mention that case because it seems to show such total absence of common sense throughout. It seems to show a deliberate avoidance of accepting the obvious. Surely if a man comes to you with an itching anus and says he wants relief, he may have sincerely desired to be rid of it. To know that such an attitude exists among consultants makes one afraid. If one was ever afflicted with a similar irritation oneself, would one ever dare seek treatment?

4

*Six Honest Serving Men for Medical Writers**

> 'I keep six honest serving men
> (They taught me all I knew);
> Their names are What and Why and When
> And How and Where and Who.
>
> *Rudyard Kipling*[1]

Kipling's poem gives an admirable summary of the way we get most of our knowledge. Most scientific enquiry is based on those six monosyllables, and the orderly presentation of a scientific paper is helped by trying to answer the six questions they pose. In this paper on the writing of articles for medical journals I shall use these six honest serving men as headings.

I am going to write as if you knew nothing about the subject and as if I knew everything, because I find it easier to write that way. In fact you are probably a capable writer yourself because the people who *can* write are usually those who read about how to do it. They are the people with well-used copies of *The Complete 'Plain Words'* by Sir Ernest Gowers[2] and Fowler's *Modern English Usage*;[3] and, if they are fortunate, Sir Clifford Albutt's *Notes on the Composition of Scientific Papers*[4] which has been out of print for a good many years. Beside the splendours of those three fine books all I write here is futile and insignificant; so you need not read this if you *can* write, but you probably will; and if you *can't* write, you ought to read this but you probably won't.

Now I return to What and Why and When and How and Where and Who.

* Written in 1968 for *The Journal of the American Medical Association* at the request of Dr Lester King.

1. *What?*

What are you going to write about? It seems obvious you should decide that first, but not everybody does. I once had an eager, but not very able young house physician who said to me, 'Oh Sir, I've decided it's about time I wrote an article. Do you agree? I thought of something about two thousand words or so. What journal do you advise me to choose? I'd be glad if you would look through it and polish it up a bit before I send it off.' I asked him what he was going to write about. 'Well, I haven't quite decided yet actually. Something fairly topical, of course. I expect you've got various bits and pieces lying around which you want working up into articles.'

He clearly looked on writing articles as a rather tedious formality to be completed in the routine of a medical career: like buying a stethoscope or registering a medical degree. I think he aimed at getting me to do most of the work for him, though I am sure he felt helpful in offering to work up my bits and pieces for me. I was amused at his attitude, but not scornful, for people who have not written articles do not realise that it takes a lot of time and trouble. They look on writing as a thing some people happen to be able to do; and, like riding a bicycle or speaking French, so easy if you can do it that you ought to be pleased to display the accomplishment. Hence that familiar approach, 'Oh, you're lucky: you can write! We'd be glad to have a contribution from you to brighten up the next issue of the Nurses Magazine.'

However, unlike my house physician, most people decide their subject before they decide to write an article. Yet I doubt if many successful authors consciously ask themselves 'What shall I write about?' More likely they get the idea 'That might be worth writing about'. When a moderate quota of experience has accumulated in the mind, and mixed there with the effects of a certain amount of informed conversation and reading, ideas are produced spontaneously if the mind is reasonably active. Once the data have been fed into the intracranial computer it ought to deliver quite a lot of ideas to its owner without further instructions.

I think that is the usual way things happen, but I cannot say much about the working of any mind but my own. Most articles I have written began with such thoughts as: 'It strikes me as rather odd that', or 'I think it needs pointing out that', or 'Nobody seems to have commented on the fact that'—fairly obvious clinical things such as a physician comes across, such as, that quite a lot of madness seemed to be caused by myxoedema, that an enormous amount of harm was done to people by keeping them too long in bed, or that people with pernicious anaemia often lost a lot of weight although they were not supposed to, and so on. I have not had difficulty in getting ideas for articles; the main problem has always been transforming ideas into articles. In fact 'What?' has troubled me much less than 'Why?' and 'When?' and 'How?' and 'Where?' and 'Who?' and the number of ideas I have had for possible articles has exceeded the number I have written. In case there are some readers who want subjects to write on I will put down some of these spare ideas in an appendix at the end of this article.

2. *Why?*

I find this the hardest question to answer. I have often thought while trying to write an article 'Why on earth am I doing this tedious and unrewarding thing?' Why, for instance, am I writing this? One reason is that I was *asked* to write it, but you don't *have* to write whenever you are asked; thank heaven for that. Flattery at being asked for an article does not play much part, because it is so hard to get a doctor to write anything that any doctor who has once succeeded in doing so is likely to be approached in case he could do it again: the standard of medical writing is so low that a doctor literate enough to put on paper something that can be read and understood without much suffering is soon looked on as a literary giant of cultured scholarship. Well then—why? I respond to the request partly because I have no good reason for refusing, and I do not want to be thought unhelpful or unobliging. As regards the lure of money I am as fond of the stuff as anybody else, but it has little effect in stimulating medical authorship because it takes such a long time to produce anything worth reading that one could earn far more in the time by caddying on the local golf course or deputising for a waiter at the local restaurant. The only strong financial incentive is for second-rate doctors to advertise themselves by reporting sensationally good results in the treatment of some widespread but intractable condition by their own new method. The lay press are always eager to seize anything sensational in the medical journals and relay it to their public in even more sensational terms.

'NEW WONDER DRUG NUGATORINE BOLONATE 221B OFFERS NEW HOPE TO ALL SUFFERERS FROM TAPANULI FEVER'

They may even take up their cudgels on behalf of such doctors, defending their specious trash against strictures and lack of support from their more ethical colleagues. Fortunately, that kind of article is not accepted by the better-class journals and anyway there are not many doctors who write that kind of thing. Our wish to have the good opinion of our colleagues is, as a rule, greater than our desire for money; or, putting it cynically—our vanity usually exceeds our avarice.

Another strong motive for writing is for the joy of seeing your own words in print. The pleasure is very great in youth but gets steadily less as you grow older. All the same, the thrill of getting the galley proofs of your first article is a genuine and glorious one. There is a notice at the top saying they must be corrected and returned by such and such a date. After carefully and eagerly correcting them you hurry off to the post with the feeling that all the Editorial Staff of *Clinical Concepts* are waiting for your article to come in and worried in case the production of that journal might be entirely disrupted if it did not arrive in time. You are slightly hurt when it does not appear in the journal till a month later, but just the same it is lovely to see it on the day. You walk into the Residency or Commonroom to see if many people are reading *Clinical Concepts*. Not quite as many as you hoped, but all of them look very absorbed. You think they are probably reading your article. Soon everybody will be discussing it. Perhaps in the next issue there will be a letter or two about your article. All this only happens the first time but it is a pleasure that you do not forget.

When Professor William Bulloch was working out the sex-linked inheritance of haemophilia he came across one article, written ten years previously, which utterly confuted his otherwise impregnable theories of its transmission: it described several women with classical haemophilia which they had inherited from their fathers. When he wrote to the author for more details he was surprised to get a reply which began 'Dear Doc'. The letter went on: 'When I wrote that article I had only just qualified, and I wanted to be sure of getting something of mine printed. So I made up some rather startling cases. I hope you won't take them too seriously.' Professor Bulloch did not take them too seriously, but this story does show that the wish to see yourself in print is not a good reason for writing an article. The best motive is the natural wish to tell others when you have noticed something unusual or interesting, or the impulse that makes a man join in a conversation when he has something to say.

3. *When?*

When to write an article? When you have something to say and you have had time to think about what you are going to say. You do not have to wait to be qualified; several first-class articles have been written by medical students.

When to write clinical records, which may be needed later? (really this applies to *all* clinical records whether or not they are likely to be used for articles). The answer is: *At the very time the observation is made*. Then you are not frustrated later by finding no record of what the cerebrospinal fluid pressure was; or worse still, tempted to invent a suitable figure for your article.

When to jot down ideas which come suddenly into your head while you are in your bath, in church, or on the top of a bus? Write them down straight away. *Do it then* (as soon as you've dried yourself, finished the hymn, or bought your ticket). Do not write them on the back of an old envelope but in a special notebook always carried for such things. In the same book you should put down other things you are likely to need later—the names and record numbers of patients of special interest, references to passages you meet when reading, or remarks you hear at medical meetings which you feel may be useful later. This will save you hours of regretful pondering: 'Where on earth did I read that excellent bit about so and so?' 'What the devil was the name of that interesting chap with such and such?' Or 'Now who was the physician at that meeting who put the surgeons so neatly in their place with that splendid remark: "The feasibility of an operation is not the best indication for its performance."?'* Of all the sound pieces of advice I have given to you this last item is the one I most earnestly wish I had always followed. I do strongly commend it to you. It may save a lot of this feeling: 'When to the sessions of sweet silent thought I summon up remembrance of things past, I sigh the lack of many a thing I sought, And with old woes new wail my dear times' waste:'[5]

* As a matter of interest it was Lord Cohen of Birkenhead.

How?

How are you going to transport the raw material in your brain into words written on paper? *How* are you going to refine the crude, unappetising result? *How*, that is in what manner or style are you going to word it?

Start by sitting at a desk with a pen and some paper. Nothing whatever happens, but the experience is valuable as it makes you realise that you have to marshal a few words in your mind before you try to write them down. You will also find that although you cannot think how to begin the article, if you start further on the beginning comes to you later.

A great deal of juggling with words and changing sentences round has to be done before you produce anything coherent. Some of this can be done in your head, but usually it is only when you see a thing written down that you think of a far better way of putting it. Use a pen or a pencil; you cannot juggle words with a dictaphone or a typewriter. I do not suppose that many American shops are old-fashioned enough to sell pen-holders and 'Relief' nibs or 'J' nibs which you dip into a bottle of ink, but they are delightful to use, and dipping the nib passes the time while you are thinking; besides that, you are able to read what you have written, which is not easy to do when you have scrawled things with a ball-point pen.

The MS you produce first will be such a mess of alterations that it is hardly fair to give it to a typist. It is kinder and better to copy it out again yourself and you will find that you can make a lot more improvements as you do so. Then, when it has been typed out, you maul it about again and get it re-typed. It is a great advantage if you can type yourself, as I have taught myself to do. If for one hour you force yourself to use the correct finger for every key, and never to look at the keyboard except when you have no idea where the wanted letter lies I promise you that you will know how to type at the end of the hour. You will be much slower than you were with two or three fingers and your eyes glued to the keyboard but if you have the will power to keep it up for a week or two you will be very glad you made the effort. And it takes only five minutes, or less, to learn the conventions about three spaces after a full stop, one after a comma and a blank line at the end of a paragraph, which will give your manuscript a professional look. Always use double or treble spacing because this leaves room for your own alterations, and later those of the Editor.

Typing the manuscript yourself gives you a proud feeling of independence, and the fact that you are about to type out a sentence makes you see its defects and remedy them before you do so.

Then you leave the manuscript to simmer in a drawer for a week or two, and when you take it out again you find that a lot of impurities have risen to the surface, and you skim them off. Repeat this as necessary and then strain the result through several layers of criticism provided by your family or your friends. (If you could get an enemy to do it that might be even better.)

Even when you have taken a lot of trouble the Editor will change a lot. You wrote about the admission of 'a young female patient of twelve years of age' and find this changed to 'a girl of twelve' and though you feel irritated you have to admit it's rather better. There may be large chunks of your MS excised, which you hardly realise until you compare the proofs with your original article. The mass excision of redundant tissue that an Editor does gives the article a better shaped body, less weighty, and moving more gracefully than the original. An author is too tender-hearted towards the fruit of his literary loins to attack them ruthlessly. Almost everyone who writes reasonably well has to slog away in the way I have described; though they often suspect that others can manage to write well without all that trouble, I don't think many can.

How to put things? This is mostly a matter of trial and error. It is more important to aim at something that reads comfortably and is easy to understand than it is to know all about fused participles, unattached gerunds and other niceties of syntax and grammar. (I am only guessing here, I do not know what either a fused participle or an unattached gerund is.) I cannot define readable, comfortable prose nor explain how to produce it. However, I can explain how *not* to put things by reaching for a current journal and choosing a muddy passage. What can I find for you now? Ah yes: this will do very well:

> Efficiency in the sense used here, means setting objectives in the use of resources in operational terms—that is in ways which can be measured—and to do this effectively information about the 'through-put' is essential if performance is to be accurately gauged.

The author is writing about efficiency in hospitals and I think he means: 'To assess efficiency you need criteria to measure it by, such as the annual turnover of patients per bed.' Now look carefully at the original version and study the seventh word, which is 'means'. Is it used with the sense 'needs' (as in 'passing exams *means* hard work') or does it imply 'has this meaning' (as in 'passing exams means succeeding in examinations')? You won't find it easy because the preceding cliché 'in the sense used here' makes certain it refers to meaning rather than to requirement, although the words which follow it make equally certain it describes requirements and not meaning, i.e. things needed to measure efficiency, rather than the meaning of the word efficiency. In fact, thc subject of that seventh word (the verb 'means') has been omitted: the sentence should have started: '*Assessing* efficiency means setting objectives . . . etc.' What with the contradictory ambiguity of the word 'means' and the omission of the subject of that verb and the muddy wording of the rest of the sentence no reader is likely to understand it and probably the author was never quite sure what he meant. I am not saying that the sentence shows any criminal disregard for language; it is sadly easy for quite careful authors to write like that. I only mentioned it to show the kind of impurity that must be cleared away if you want to write something good. If you leave such things clogging an article it will not excite much criticism or get you into trouble any more than it will if you show lantern slides no one can read (except a few people in the front row with telescopes). The standard of medical writers and lecturers has hardened people to that sort of thing. Yet if you *can* take the trouble to give people something better, some of them may be a little grateful.

Routine medical jargon is never very pleasant to swallow. Here is the poem with which I opened this article, first put down as Kipling originally wrote it and then re-written as if it was intended for a medical journal.

First version

I keep six honest serving men
(They taught me all I knew);
Their names are What and Why and When
And How and Where and Who.

Second version

Hypercuriosis elefantorum infantis
(extracted from *Proc. Paed. Pachyderm.*)

SUMMARY

A survey of the writer's personal methodology in the technique of general enquiry has been carried out. The results have been analysed to determine the principal components of his interrogatory system. Six distinct forms of question have been isolated as tabulated below. It is claimed that the responses elicited by these were responsible for the total quantity of the author's knowledge.

TABLE II *The Established Questionary*

(broken down to show main orientation of responses desired)

Number of Question	Short Title	Orientation and Purposed Objective of Question
1	What?	Nature of referent to be established
2	Why?	Determination of underlying motivation
3	When?	Time sequence and Chronological Placement
4	How?	Analysis of Technique and Method Assay
5	Where?	Determination of Spatial Relationships
6	Who?	Identification of Personnel Concerned

I wonder which version you prefer.

5. *Where?*

Where to write it? In any place where you feel comfortable doing so. Some people like the television blaring away and children climbing over them, and others do not. The early stages can be managed comfortably in an armchair with a board about ten by twelve inches to write on. Later stages go better in a more disciplined position at a desk. But wherever you are there should be a dictionary within easy reach. If you get the smallest twinge of uncertainty about the meaning or the spelling of a word you ought to look it up. If you are just going to write 'I view this prospect with considerable temerity' and you suspect the last word may not mean quite what you hope it does—a dictionary will tell you that it doesn't. Or you are certain how to spell always, although and almost but you wonder if 'alright' is all right—you will find it isn't. Though sure of 'someone' and 'anyone' you may have doubts of 'noone', which are justified. (I always spelt it like that until a friend laughingly read it aloud to rhyme with loony.) Though Editors and printers put most of that kind of mistake right they do not enjoy the extra work and the more errors there are the greater are the chances of some of them slipping through. It is very easy to make mistakes over the difference between practise and practice (thinking of advise and advice may help you) and also between mucus and mucous, ilium and ileum, and principle and principal. About one doctor in three spells all the ϕ θ words without their first h: diptheria instead of diphtheria—ophthalmoscope—phthisis and so on: a full quota of H's lends a cultured tone to your MS even though you may not have done Greek at School.

Where did that come from? (reference, quotation or extract). References are given in case the reader wants to look them up, not to show him what a lot you have read. Many of the enormous lists of references you meet are concocted by assembling several prefabricated collections from other works but without reading any of the articles they refer to (as shown by the persistence of unnoticed errors in them). It is a flashy practice to muster these braggart mammoths.

However good your memory is, you should look up everything you quote. You may be certain there is a book called Alice in Wonderland, and that it mentions a Mad Hatter; that there is another Alice book called Alice Through the Looking-Glass and that Sherlock Holmes said 'Elementary my dear Watson' and also that an apple is mentioned in the Bible story of Adam and Eve in the Garden of Eden: in all those five cases you are wrong.[6]

Where will your article be published? In the most reputable journal which takes your kind of article, or failing that—the next most reputable. And only in one place please: do not serve up the same article, re-hashed and disguised, every two or three years. For money-making pot-boilers write for the glossy pharmaceuticals, and use them, too, when you want a lot of coloured photographs printed which the other journals can't afford.

For letting off steam and entertaining others—write fiery letters in the correspondence columns of the medical journals on perennially controversial subjects: organ transplants, enuresis, contraception, psychosomatic and/or social medicine, tonsillectomy and psychiatrists; or fire a salvo among the combatants already fighting there. Sometimes you should write for your own hospital magazine, but if you write something rather good you may wish later you had kept it for a journal with a wider circulation.

6. *Who?*

Who wrote the article? You did, of course, so do not list as co-authors a host of people who never wrote a word of it; if they helped in other ways thank them at the end of the article. I once let a colleague who was gathering facts for an article use a few of my case-records and I had compulsory co-authorship thrust on me afterwards. I tried to stop him but I couldn't. Later on I tried to read the article but I couldn't.

The authors listed at the head of an article should be the people who actually wrote it. Two people, and possibly three can write an article: but no more than that. Six people can no more write an article than they could all drive a car simultaneously. Crowds of spurious authors confuse the reader and make reference work harder for him.

I was told when I visited America, that it is a common thing for a young author to write every word of an article himself but be compelled to name the Head of his Department as the chief author so that he can get free reprints. I hope that is not true, it sounds a dreadful arrangement. Heads of departments may provide inspiration, encouragement and example but surely it is better to reward them with a polite acknowledgement at the end instead of a downright lie at the beginning.

Who gets reprints sent to him by the author. That is for the author to decide, especially if he is not getting them free. If there are not many to spare he will naturally give them to the people who write and ask for them. I think those printed request cards are horrible. Departmental tycoons proclaim 'File all literature on *XYZ*'! and then their secretaries rake the globe with printed cards gathering a hoard of reprints which are interred in the tycoon's private mausoleum (without being read, I suspect). As it takes a man at least five minutes to read an article he should be able to spend half a minute writing for it. In my experience the best people usually do, e.g. Presidents of Colleges as opposed to Departmental Tycoons. It will be interesting to see how many printed request cards I get asking for reprints of this article because they can only come from people who have not read as far as this.

Finally, the Who of: '*Who* is this fellow?' '*Who* does he think he is?' The fear of arousing such criticisms often troubles authors. A writer sometimes worries more about what people will think of him than about what they will think of his article. However, a man writes less effectively if he is working part-time as his own public relations officer. It is best to write entirely 'uncowed by fear or favour of the crowd' but I doubt if there are many people who can manage to do so. You *ought* to write neither to please nor to provoke, neither to conform nor to confute but solely to convey. Your object is not to be thought a nice chap, but to write a good article. Many of the finest writers are not nice chaps, and plenty of nice chaps write atrociously.

I conclude by adapting some lines by Hilaire Belloc[7] to express a sincere hope of my own which is probably the real reason why I have written this article:

When I am dead, I hope it may be said
His sins were scarlet but his words were read.

REFERENCES AND EXPLANATIONS

1. Kipling, R. (1902) 'The Elephant's Child.' *Just So Stories.* Macmillan & Co.
2. Gowers, E. (1954) *The Complete Plain Words.* H.M. Stationery Office. (Now issued as a Penguin.)
3. Fowler, H. W. (1965) *A Dictionary of Modern English Usage.* Oxford, at the Clarendon Press.
4. Allbutt, T. C. (1925) *Notes on the Composition of Scientific Papers.* Macmillan & Co.
5. Shakespeare, W. (*c.* 1590) *Sonnets.* No. 30. First four lines.
6. Lewis Carroll's famous book is not called Alice in Wonderland but *Alice's Adventures in Wonderland*. It never refers to The Mad Hatter but only to The Hatter. The doubts about the Hatter's sanity arise from (*a*) A neighbour's statement 'He is mad' which carries little weight as it was made by an unstable Cheshire Cat with no recorded psychiatric qualifications, and (*b*) The expression 'Mad as a Hatter' which is derived from 'Mad as an Adder' and so reflects only upon the common viper Pelias Berus and not upon the incidence of industrial mercuric nitrate poisoning ('Hatter's Shakes') which can cause psychoses. The other Alice book is: *Through the Looking-Glass* not Alice Through the Looking-Glass. The Holmes passage runs, 'Excellent' said I. 'Elementary' said he. Finally, there are no apples mentioned in Genesis—only 'fruit'.
7. Belloc, H. (*c.* 1930) Epigrams—'On His Books' (the original has 'books' not 'words').

APPENDIX

(Some ideas for possible articles)

Anybody who wants to use any of these is welcome to do so and without any acknowledgement.

1. *The Medical Abdomen*

A collection of case histories of patients with entirely medical conditions which presented as 'acute surgical abdomen'. Not just a catalogue of the illnesses which traditionally do this, but, collected over the years the records of patients who really did present in this way.

I made a collection some years ago (which I never published) which included shingles (before the rash came), hepatitis (before the jaundice showed), pneumonia, acute pyelitis, Addison's disease, haematoporphyrinuria, diabetic coma, tabetic crisis and others. An article founded wholly upon genuine case histories describes only what *does* happen and leaves out what is supposed to happen; moreover, the genuine case so often is enlivened by some individual oddity: for example the child with diabetic pre-coma whose abdominal pain therefrom had been mistaken for acute appendicitis; as she was coming round from the anaesthetic after the normal appendix had been removed she vomited over the anaesthetist who complained of the reek of acetone, and it was that which made people realise the urine had not been tested. Nobody is proud of such things, but recording them does provide what Pooh Bah described as 'Merely corroborative detail, intended to give artistic verisimilitude to an otherwise bald and unconvincing narrative'.[8]

2. *Queer Turns*

This expression may not be used much in America, but in England it is common for people to complain of 'queer turns', 'black-outs' or attacks of 'coming over queer' when they have suffered from recurrent, brief alterations of consciousness with feelings of strangeness and confusion. There is a very large variety of conditions which can produce this symptom—postural hypotension, syncope, minor epilepsy, Stokes Adams attacks, spontaneous hypoglycaemia, paroxysmal tachycardia, labyrinthine disease, phaeochromocytoma—and in the elderly those minor strokes, so mild as to be dismissed as just a 'queer turn' which commonly precede a major stroke. (People still argue whether transient cerebrovascular spasm or very small thrombi are responsible and nobody seems to know.)

In many 'queer turns' a firm diagnosis is never made: no doubt a certain proportion have emotional rather than organic origins. However, the condition is quite common and if a collection of such cases was gathered over several years and followed up thoroughly it would provide the material for a most valuable dissertation on the various causes which accounted for them, how these were established and what proportion were never diagnosed.

3. *Reversal Syndromes* (*or Rebound Syndromes*)

I cannot think of a good name for this important but un-named trouble, but I will try to explain what I am talking about. I think you will recognise it, and perhaps you can think of a better name for it.

Fits occur quite commonly when barbiturate addicts have their supplies suddenly cut off, although they are not epileptics. The same thing happens with alcoholics. Myxoedema will often develop in a euthyroid woman who has been unjustifiably kept on big doses of thyroxine for many months when it is stopped. (That is why it is so wicked to hand out huge amounts of thyroid to non-myxoedematous fat ladies as many people do.) Similarly, the failure of the adrenal cortex after cortisone treatment is becoming well known, and quite often this has a fatal outcome when doctors forget about it; the adrenal cortex with even more alacrity than the thyroid gland will retire from work if the dispensary takes over its job for a little while. The islet cells of the pancreas behave likewise and fail to meet a large demand for insulin when previous requirements have been small (that is: a man who has eaten hardly any carbohydrate for several months will develop glycosuria if he suddenly takes a lot). Contrariwise, in a carbohydrate glutton a sudden abstinence from carbohydrate (especially if assisted by exertion which uses up the little there is) can produce quite severe hypoglycaemia.

I have said enough for you to know what I mean, and I think you will. The subject is really quite large and important and you could find many other examples of it. You might even dose yourself with big amounts of iron for a goodish while and see if you got a transient iron-deficiency when you stopped; then you could go on to see if you could achieve a megaloblastic blood picture by a similar experiment with cyanocobalamine. And so on.

The next three subjects I list depend on clinical observations of mine which, being only impressions may be without foundation, though I feel fairly sure they are not.

4. *Complexion in Treated Pernicious Anaemia*

I often noticed that the proportion of people with noticeably ruddy complexions was much higher among those with treated pernicious anaemia than among other patients with equally high blood counts. The point could easily be settled merely by getting someone who had no idea which patients were which to classify their complexions as pale, normal, or ruddy.

5. *Paranoia with Deafness*

The incidence of deafness in people with paranoia seems remarkably high. A likely explanation could be that it is much easier to think people are talking about you if you don't know what they are saying (as you may have noticed when travelling in a railway carriage in a foreign country). Obviously, if deafness is related to paranoid delusions it is the more important for hearing aids to be started early, before one affliction is supplemented by the other.

6. *Vomiting caused by Stokes Adams Attacks*

I have had two patients who had repeated attacks of very severe vomiting which were caused by Stokes Adams attacks. Only because their wives described pallor followed by a flushing of the face when they recovered did the possibility of this diagnosis occur to me. I had no idea that vomiting was ever a feature of Stokes Adams attacks till then. When I looked up the matter I found that Thomas Spens gave a vivid description of it when he described these attacks half a century before Stokes or Adams had written about them,[9] and so did Sir William Burnett thirty years later.[10] I do not think nowadays it is recognised that vomiting attacks of great severity may occur in heart block, so if you meet one or two cases you could write a very useful paper on this subject.

There are six suggestions for papers by physicians and now I will put two for surgeons.

7. *When to Take out Stitches?*

Many a good article has been written by attacking firmly established traditions which lack the security of rational foundations. Certainly the tradition as to the particular day stitches should be removed needs to have its foundations inspected because the number of days decreed for stitches to stay in varies widely among different surgeons, and various hospitals and countries each have their own traditional custom.

Has any serious research been done to find how early stitches have to be taken out for wounds to gape as a result. Although plastic surgeons take out stitches on the fourth day or earlier, abdominal stitches are usually kept in till the tenth day. Why? They don't hold anything except the skin do they? The other layers are tied separately. Do surgeons really believe that the belly might burst open if they were taken out too soon? A layman might well believe that, but for a surgeon to think so would be 'a travesty of reasoning that should not have survived the discipline of a scientific education'.* Look through records of people who burst open after abdominal surgery and see if their stitches were removed earlier than from those who did not. I think you will find that the calamity only developed in those with severe coughs who were fat, old or feeble, and did not show any relationship with the date the stitches came out.

8. *The Use of Cotton for Sutures*

Is there any real need for all the elaborate, difficult-to-sterilise and potentially hazardous materials used for sutures? Cotton is cheap, it is not harmed by boiling, which makes it easy to sterilise, and it holds the first half of a knot without slipping. During the war, when it was used a lot, all the sutures for a partial gastrectomy operation came to less than one penny. It is not safe for bladder operations because, not being absorbed, it may form the nucleus of a stone, but otherwise there is a lot to be said for it.

That completes eight suggestions which I bequeathe to you with my best wishes. I will now advise you what not to write.

Do not Write

Please do not write any more articles about cholesterol and coronary disease and the diet and drugs which are supposed to influence them. The facts about coronary disease are these: the less atheromatous your ancestors, the harder your water, and the more habitual exercise you take, the less likely you are to be troubled by it. Do stop bothering about whether your fats are saturated or unsaturated, help yourselves liberally to butter and stop propagating these erroneous legends.

A final warning: when—rather late in life—you have the great honour of delivering the Aesculepian Oration for 1984; even though your faculties may be starting to fail by then, do remember that it is *not* obligatory to speak on: 'Whither Medicine Today?', 'The Art of Medicine in The Future', or 'The Changing Face of Modern Medicine'. Nor is it essential to begin your oration with: 'The last few decades of this century have witnessed an almost unprecedented and bewildering series of therapeutic and diagnostic advances. The discovery of sulphonamides and antibiotics has ushered in a new era of treatment, and the daily advances in the complexity and sophistication of modern blah blah blah—and so on.' All that has been done before. And a jolly sight too often, too!

* An expression I stole from Sir Francis Walshe.

Well, what *can* you do if they make you an Orator? Here is one subject which would be all right—Atmosphere. I do not mean what you breathe but what makes one hospital pleasant and another hospital unpleasant. It is the most valuable thing any hospital can possess and yet very little has been said about its ingredients. They are numerous and interesting: front-hall porters, newspaper boys and ward maids contribute much to it, depending on whether they are alert, polite, cheerful and friendly or not. The telephone operators of the hospital switchboard play an enormous part. These matters do far more for a hospital than a new electronic machine for scanning Rorsach responses. A large number of notices telling people all the things they *must not* do and warning them it is their fault if their property gets stolen, and a few gum-chewing attendants with soiled uniforms do more harm to a hospital than one missed diagnosis of pseudo-pseudo-spontaneous hypoparathyroidism. The subject of hospital atmosphere is vast, and a man with wisdom and the gift of handling words well could make a splendid oration on it.

APPENDIX REFERENCES

8. Gilbert, W. S. *The Mikado* Act. II.
9. Spens, T. (1793) *Medical Commentaries* vii, 463 Edinburgh.
10. Burnett, W. (1827) *Med- Chir. Trans.*, xiii, 202 (paper read 1824).

5

*The Seven Sins of Medicine**

There is an unlimited number of medical sins, but I am going to catalogue and comment on seven of them in the hope that those students who wish to avoid them may do so and those who wish to indulge in them may enlarge their repertoire or refine their technique. The seven sins are obscurity, cruelty, bad manners, over-specialisation, love of the rare, stupidity, and sloth.

OBSCURITY

Both in writing and in lecturing clear style and short words are best. Obscurity is bad, not only because it is difficult to understand but also because it is confused with profundity, just as a shallow muddy pool may look deep. Here is an example from a recent article. The writers wanted to say: 'We judge men's health by their working-places and their homes', but they imbedded their meaning in this sentence: 'It is generally accepted that the evaluation of the nutritional status of a community should include assessments of the environmental conditions under which individual members live and work.' As Mr Ivor Brown[1] has pointed out, such writing produces a slow weak ooze of words instead of a keen forceful jet. The double negative is a common way of making a simple statement harder to understand, and if we read 'It is by no means far from infrequently that the absence of tubercle bacilli is not invariably detected', few of us can say whether tubercle bacilli are present or not (nor do we care).

I warn students taking histories against turning the simple English of their patients into the jargon of their textbooks. If a patient says 'if I go half-way up a hill I feel I'm done for', these very words should

* A lecture given to the University College Hospital Medical Society on 17 March 1948, and published in *The Lancet* in August 1949.

appear in the notes rather than 'The patient complains that during ambulation up a moderate incline he suffers a feeling of impending dissolution'.

CRUELTY

Cruelty is probably the most important and prevalent sin in the list I have chosen. Usually it is due to thoughtlessness, and not deliberate. *Mental cruelty* is common and arises in three ways: (1) by saying too much; (2) by saying too little; and (3) by the patient being forgotten. By saying too much we often burden a patient with a load of anxiety which adds to the illness we are trying to relieve. Many times I have seen patients who felt well till they were told they had high blood-pressure or a heart murmur, and since that time have been afflicted with every grievous symptom which could be gathered from hearsay, from patent medicine advertisements, and from 'The Home Doctor'. Before telling a patient anything of his illness it is essential to consider whether it will help him or harm him, and with a little practice one soon learns what it is wise to say.

By saying too little one can cause the fear of the unknown; the gaps may be filled in by the patient with alarming inventions and superstitions. That is why some explanation should be given to the patient who is discharged from hospital, both so that some of his groundless fears are removed and so that if he gets under the care of another doctor he can give a moderately accurate account of what he has had. The doctor should know what fears and superstitions are common among patients so that he may allay them and prevent mental cruelty. For example, a patient with shingles has nearly always been told by his grandmother that 'if they meet in the middle you die', and the assurance that neither will they meet nor will he die may give him much relief. Patients with mild arthritis are usually terrified of becoming 'crippled with rheumatism', and, similarly, many patients with bronchitis dread tuberculosis; in these cases reassurance is more important than medicine, and it is the doctor's duty to dig out these fears if possible.

Lastly, forgetting the patient. I refer to that kind of bedside teaching and discussion where the patient is treated as if he were unconscious, or discussed as if he already lay on the necropsy slab. It must be remembered that patients have ears, and that sotto-voice murmurings about polysyllabic diseases strike needless terror into their hearts.

Physical Cruelty

Over-investigation is a form of physical cruelty. If a man is dying of secondary cancer and the primary cancer will soon be discovered at necropsy, it is cruel to make his last days uncomfortable by playing at 'hunt the primary' as one might play 'hunt the slipper', and it gives extra work to the radiologists and pathologists. Patients dying of heart-failure are happier without cardiac catheters, arterial punctures, and other tests beloved of those who judge a patient with heart-failure by his cardiac output in litres per minute rather than by the number of stairs he can climb.

Here are some minor cruelties which can easily be avoided. Do not give mersalyl in the evening, so keeping the patient awake passing urine all night. Do not do a fractional test-meal on a patient with pernicious anaemia when he is admitted with a haemoglobin in the twenties; put his haemoglobin up with liver treatment first—his achlorhydria will keep. Do not play at 'pushing the parkinsonian'; there are enough signs of parkinsonism to diagnose a case without pushing him in the back to see how far he totters forward. Do not put sticking plaster on hairy limbs; you can easily shave them first. Do not wheel elaborate trolleys to a patient's bedside and start sticking needles in him until you have given him a word of reassurance and explanation.

BAD MANNERS

If students do not learn good manners while they are learning medicine they will be at a great disadvantage in dealing with patients, nurses, and colleagues.

Towards Patients. I once asked a student to examine the abdomen of a patient lying in an outpatient cubicle. He dashed into the cubicle where she lay, flung back the blanket, plumped his hand on her abdomen, shouted 'Gosh, what a beauty' (he was referring to the patient's enlarged spleen and not to her personal appearance), and dashed out again. Such behaviour must be condemned.

Other forms of bad manners are: (1) impatience in taking a history from a slow-witted patient; (2) making jokes at the expense of the patient; and (3) reading the patient's newspaper which lies on his bed and displays headlines far more exciting than the story the patient is telling.

Towards Nurses. Students will find that a courteous good morning to the sisters makes their access to patients and to ward equipment much easier. (In America the remark 'Good morning, sister', is equivalent to saying 'How goes it, honey?' and should be avoided.) Too many students or house-men call for a nurse in the manner of an impatient diner calling for a waiter.

Towards Medical Staff. Years ago a student would take his hands out of his pockets even if a registrar passed him, and almost grovel at the sight of a chief. Perhaps the senior staff had too much majesty and pomp in those days, but the pendulum has swung in the other direction today. At any rate, I advise students not to examine an abdomen with one hand in the pocket, because it is an inefficient way of palpating; it will irritate physicians and give a bad impression in the examination hall. In general, students should aim at a reasonable respect for their seniors but avoid an oily deference. I further caution them against bad manners when they become more senior, and suggest such courtesies as asking their colleagues' permission before seeing a case in their wards, and writing and congratulating them on their publications or appointments.

OVER-SPECIALISATION

It is right that a doctor should have special interest and knowledge about one subject. It is wrong for him to show special indifference and ignorance about all other subjects. A good doctor should be a jack-of-all-trades and master of one. For example, a surgeon should be able to advise a patient with simple obesity about her diet and not refer her to an endocrine clinic; a gynaecologist should be capable of treating a mild iron-deficiency anaemia without referring her to an anaemia clinic; and a physician ought to squash a small ganglion on the back of the hand with his thumbs (or bible). I have known an eye surgeon after seeing a case of retinitis pigmentosa write in the notes: 'This might be part of the Laurence-Moon-Biedl syndrome; is there any evidence of polydactyly?' For an ophthalmologist to feel himself incapable of counting fingers is surely the limit of over-specialisation; and, if nothing is done to stop this tendency, we shall have one physician who specialises in the first heart sound, and the other who is only concerned with the second.

Perhaps the worst feature of specialisation is that it makes doctors feel they are doing wrong to deal with even the simplest case if it lies within the protected area of somebody else's specialty. Particularly is this the case with psychiatry, which is regarded by other doctors with a mixture of suspicion, reverence, and ridicule. In Noel Coward's *Blithe Spirit* a character, referring to psychotherapy, says: 'I refuse to go through months of expensive humiliation in order to find that at the age of ten I was desperately in love with my rocking-horse.' A surgeon or a physician faced with a patient exhibiting some 'functional' symptoms is likely to take a similar attitude, feeling that the origin of the simplest psychoneurotic symptoms lies buried in an uncharted swamp in which only the expert can poke with impunity—a swamp crawling with complexes and repressions, where nothing is what it seems and everything symbolises something indecent. This is a foolish attitude to take; a sensible physician or surgeon should be able to give wise counsel in the simpler case of neurosis.

Further, there is a complication of specialisation—that it allows bees to remain undisturbed within their masters' bonnets so that the allergist looks at the world through allergic-coloured glasses and beams myopically at a world where everything is allergic.

LOVE OF THE RARE (SPANOPHILIA)

This sin is more prevalent among students, because they lack the experience that teaches which illnesses are common and which are rare. It is responsible for the failure of bookworms to pass exams. Headache and vomiting are more often due to migraine than to cerebral tumour; nose-bleeding is more often due to picking the nose than to multiple hereditary haemorrhagic telangiectasis; and wasting of the small muscles of the hand occurs in old age and rheumatoid arthritis more often than in motor-neurone disease or cervical rib.

COMMON STUPIDITY

By this I mean the opposite of common sense—common nonsense in fact. There are many kinds of this particular sin, but I think the commonest type is what might be called therapeutic automatism. No illness has a rigid code of treatment which must be advised in all circumstances; one must cut one's therapeutic coat according to the mental and economic cloth of one's patient. It is mere foolishness to order an elaborate diet for a busy working-class woman with instructions to add on the fourth day $1\frac{3}{4}$ oz of steamed red mullet to the graduated scheme prescribed. I saw the finest example of therapeutic automatism as a medical student when I was skating one winter on the local squire's pond, watching all the quality displaying their skill. A woman fell and broke her tibia. I longed to treat her, but I was only a student. 'She mustn't be moved till the doctor comes; we must treat her for shock', cried all the bystanders. It was only at the last moment that these zealous first-aiders were persuaded to abandon their treatment and drag the lady off the ice; otherwise the patient, together with a valuable collection of furs, might have been lost.* I mention this to show that patients should never be treated by rote and rule, for there may be special circumstances.

SLOTH

Medical sloth can be physical or mental. Physical sloth exists more than we like to admit. When bloodbanks and standard apparatus made transfusion quick and easy, the number of transfusions quadrupled in a few years, which makes it regrettably apparent that the easiness of treatment rather than its urgency may decide whether or not it is given.

Physical Sloth

This often causes the omission of blood-pressure estimations, ophthalmoscopy, or rectal examination, and leads to lapses in aseptic ritual (if a lumbar-puncture needle touches the bed-clothes, it is tempting to pretend not to notice it). Physical sloth may also affect the overworked nurse who, tired of counting respirations, adds one more twenty to the row of twenties already on the chart, and this may stretch the doctor's powers of belief greatly.

Mental Sloth

This is commoner and more important. Especially in history-taking is sloth the great danger. If the day is hot, the patient deaf, the doctor in a hurry, and the history garnished with reminiscences and irrelevances, it requires enormous patience and concentration to distil the essence from it. One form of unconscious sloth is worth special mention. Do not accept the patient's diagnosis when taking a history—find out his symptoms. Rheumatic fever at the age of 10 years is important, but the patient's statement that he had it needs amplification. He may have been one day in bed with a pain in the ankle which his aunt said was rheumatic fever or, on the other hand, may have been twelve weeks in bed with flitting joint pains of great severity starting after a sore throat. Similarly with diet (so important a part of

* The full story of this incident is recorded on page 52 of this book.

the history in cases of anaemia), do not write 'adequate' or 'fair', but find out what exactly your patient eats at each meal, and you will be astonished how many women are living on bread and margarine and countless cups of tea.

Lastly, beware of sloth in thinking. If you are too lazy to think for yourselves, you will fall an easy prey to the less thoughtful papers and publications, blindly accepting the myth and mumpsimus against which John Forbes[2] has so ably warned us. If you cultivate a healthy doubt (without being unduly sceptical) you may have the experience of the Queen of the Fairies in *Iolanthe*:

'On fire that glows
With heat intense
I turn the hose
Of common sense
And out it goes
At small expense.'

Please adopt this attitude with everything I have said, and realise that much of it may be nonsense.

REFERENCES

1. *Just Another Word* (1943) London.
2. Forbes, J. R. (1946) *Lancet*, ii, 293.

6

*Myxoedematous Madness**

Myxoedema is one of the most important, one of the least known, and one of the most frequently missed causes of organic psychoses—important because it may respond so gratifyingly to treatment, little known because little has been written about it, often missed because the textbook description of myxoedema is not the rule but the exception.

Fourteen cases are here described, all of which had myxoedema and psychotic changes. In every one of them the diagnosis was confirmed beyond doubt. They all showed a psychosis amounting to complete 'madness', ten being admitted to the mental observation wards under the Lunacy Act, one referred to the neurosurgeon for cerebral tumour, and three to general medical wards with other diagnoses. In nine of the cases there was a dramatic and complete recovery of sanity with thyroid treatment, in two there was partial improvement, one showed no change, and two patients died. The fact that in none of these cases had the diagnosis been made by the outside doctor suggests that there is need for increased awareness of myxoedema as a cause of psychoses, and, further, shows that it may be worth while discussing how myxoedema can be diagnosed so that cases may be recognised and treated early.

The average doctor is well aware that dullness and a poor memory are caused by myxoedema, but does not realise that a frank psychosis can occur. Dr Leonard Simpson, in Price's *Medicine*, describes the condition clearly and stresses its importance, but most of the popular textbooks omit any reference to it at all, and this may account for the rarity of its recognition. Apart from medical textbooks, A. J. Cronin (1937) paints a vivid if sensational picture of a 'mad myxoedema', and it was from this source that I first learned of the

* Published in the *British Medical Journal*, 10 September 1949.

condition. Though Stoll (1932) described six personal cases, the fact that Zondek and Wolfsohn (1944) published one solitary case of myxoedematous psychosis in 1944 suggests again that it is regarded as a rarity. Nevertheless, the condition was clearly described, and was recognised as exceedingly common by the Committee of the Clinical Society of London (1888) appointed in 1883 to consider the subject of myxoedema. Their report says (p. 31): 'Delusions and hallucinations occur in nearly half the cases, mainly where the disease is advanced. Insanity as a complication is noted in about the same proportion as delusions and hallucinations. It takes the form of acute or chronic manias, dementia, or melancholia, with a marked predominance of suspicion and self-accusation.' (At the time of that report thyroid treatment was quite unknown, so doubtless many of the cases would to-day have been diagnosed and treated before mental symptoms arose.) I want to make it clear that I am not describing something new, but something old that is nowadays often forgotten.

IS THERE A SPECIFIC TYPE OF PSYCHOSIS ASSOCIATED WITH MYXOEDEMA?

This question is fully discussed by Akelaitis (1936). The possible theories are: (1) that myxoedema produces a psychosis depending on the 'pre-psychotic reaction type'; (2) that it produces a specific type of psychosis; and (3) that it produces psychoses of various types, either resembling one of the ordinary idiopathic psychoses or else typical of no special type.

Cases in the literature record a very wide variety of mental changes, and certainly in the series I have observed there has been no constant type of psychosis, though general confusion and disorientation with persecutory delusions and hallucinations, and occasional bouts of restless violence, have been common. I have made the diagnosis on the myxoedematous appearance of the patient and not on the kind of mental symptoms. No physician would attempt to diagnose lobar pneumonia or typhoid by the delirium they may produce, and likewise in myxoedema it is the disease which is the characteristic feature, not its mental manifestations.

The fact that recorded cases of myxoedema psychosis have closely resembled paranoia (Case 1 and Stoll, 1932), schizophrenia (Zondek and Wolfsohn, 1944), melancholia (Buschan, 1896), or other orthodox psychoses does suggest that the common psychoses—schizophrenia, mania, melancholia, paranoia, and so on may turn out to be not diagnoses in themselves, but manifestations of underlying organic disease.

DOES THE RESPONSE TO THYROID PROVE THE MYXOEDEMATOUS ORIGIN OF THE PSYCHOSIS?

First, if the case responds it is of course no absolute proof, because almost any type of psychosis can improve spontaneously. Nevertheless, when mental symptoms that have been present in a hypothyroid patient for many months clear dramatically within a few weeks of starting thyroid it is reasonably certain that they were due to myxoedema.

Secondly, if the mental changes persist after adequate thyroid treatment, does this mean they were not myxoedematous? As Ruhberg (1936) points out: 'It is necessary to determine if they are secondary to thyroid insufficiency or merely a coincident concomitant'. He states dogmatically: 'If the mental symptoms are part of myxoedema, improvement and relief should be obtained by establishing a normal basal metabolic rate'. Akelaitis (1936), discussing cases which showed physical but not mental improvement with thyroid, also concludes: 'The psychosis was a coincidence and not part of the myxoedema'. Such dogmatic assumptions are unjustified. It is generally agreed that metabolic changes can produce irreversible damage; for instance, the changes of prolonged hypoglycaemia or of pellagra may fail to respond respectively to glucose or to the vitamin B complex, although they were caused by deprivations of these. Again, the belated treatment of cretinism shows that the changes in the brain cannot be reversed by thyroid.

Dr Leonard Simpson (personal communication) records such a case in which peculiar behaviour persisted after thyroid treatment and ultimately ended in psychosis. Hence prolonged thyroid deficiency may well cause a psychotic change which does not respond to thyroid. I believe that myxoedema, if left untreated, can produce an incurable psychosis, and I consider that those cases that have not been completely cured (Cases 1, 2, and 8) with thyroid were nevertheless initially caused by lack of thyroid, especially as two of them improved a great deal at the beginning of treatment.

I can give no certain evidence (from analysing these fourteen cases) that the longer the myxoedema is left untreated the poorer is the outlook for recovery, though this is what one would expect.

It is so hard to determine when the myxoedema started that one can only guess at the answer.

Case 1

A housewife aged 55 was admitted on an authorised officer's order on Aug. 26, 1944, confused, hallucinated, and with persecutory ideas. Fourteen years previously she took her child to another hospital with a whitlow. The casualty officer, noticing that she herself looked thyrotoxic, referred her to a surgeon. Total thyroidectomy was performed. On discharge she was instructed to take thyroid, but stopped doing so after five years. She had thus been without thyroid for the nine years preceding her admission. For three years her daughters had noticed her increasing deafness, hoarseness of voice, and mental strangeness. She believed neighbours and others were plotting to harm her; she heard imaginary voices, and sometimes expressed delusions of grandeur.

On examination she was seen to be mentally retarded, apathetic, and sluggish. Occasionally, she would become excited and complain of hearing voices or that the nursing staff was plotting to kill her. She was so confused and disorientated that she was unable to give an account of herself. She had the typical appearance of advanced myxoedema with gross non-pitting oedema of the whole body. She had well-marked supraclavicular pads, scanty eyebrows, thick croaking voice, and dry scaly skin. She was slow and ponderous in both body and mind. Her pulse was 65 and the blood cholesterol 362 mg/100 ml; it was not possible to take the basal metabolic rate.

In addition to myxoedema she had gross elephantiasis of the left leg with scars of a previous Kondoleon operation. This elephantiasis had come on rapidly eight years previously. At the time of the operation (four years previously at another hospital) the house-surgeon, after describing the leg, records: 'whole body now solid with lymphatic oedema'. This suggests that she was really grossly myxoedematous at that time, but that because she had lymphatic oedema of the leg the generalised swelling was incorrectly assumed to be lymphatic oedema also.

Progress. She was treated with 1 gr (65 mg) of thyroid four times daily, increasing by 1 gr a day till she was taking 8 gr (0·52 g) daily. The blood cholesterol came down as follows: Aug. 29, 362 mg/100 ml; Sept. 5, 354 mg; Sept. 18, 230 mg; Sept. 26, 158 mg. The thyroid was then reduced to 1 gr four times daily, whereupon the cholesterol rose to 273 mg by Oct. 13. The thyroid was again increased to 2 gr (0·13 g) four times daily and the cholesterol came down again; thus on Oct. 24 it was 225 mg and on Nov. 7 163 mg. It therefore seemed that she required this large dose of 8 gr a day, and, having had a *total* thyroidectomy, this was not surprising. During treatment her physical improvement was slow and her mental improvement disappointing. After six weeks she had lost 7 lb (3·18 kg) in weight and her appearance was noticeably less myxoedematous. Mentally there was an increase in alertness and sufficient decrease in disorientation and noisiness for her to be transferred from the mental observation ward to a general medical ward on Oct. 19; but she continued (though less constantly) to behave peculiarly and she had to be sent back to the observation ward on Nov. 6. Three months after admission (Nov. 28) she had lost over 14 lb (6·35 kg) in weight and the improvement in her appearance was more apparent, but as she did not show any further mental improvement she was transferred to Shenley Mental Hospital. Though she still thought other patients were making accusations against her and stated that she and King George VI jointly owned the hospital, there was a great improvement compared with her mental state on admission, for she could give a full account of her previous history and was far less confused.

Case 2

A housewife aged 60 was admitted on an authorised officer's order on Dec. 20, 1945, with delusions of persecution and hallucinations. For six months she had noticed that her voice was croaking and she felt cold weather badly, but she had noted no other myxoedematous symptoms—no gain in weight, falling out of hair, or deafness. During the week before admission she had an idea that her landlord was trying to poison her 'because she knew all about the shootings in the back garden'. She heard voices talking to her continuously, and locked herself in her room to protect herself from imaginary enemies.

On examination she was completely confused and disorientated, and showed the delusions and hallucinations described above. Her appearance was that of advanced myxoedema, with puffy face, malar flush, toad-like skin, scanty hair, and croaking nasal voice. She slept a great deal, with unusually sonorous snoring. The pulse was 60, cholesterol 374 mg/100 ml, basal metabolic rate −26 per cent, blood pressure 170/90.

Progress. She was treated with 1 gr of thyroid thrice daily, starting on Dec. 24. She made steady improvement, both mental and physical: after a week she lost her delusions and realised that they had been absurd. After a fortnight she was rational, orientated, and almost completely clear. After three weeks she had lost 14 lb (6·35 kg) in weight and now slept without snoring. (This was a particularly striking feature of the case.) Her appearance was much improved and the blood cholesterol had come down from 374 to 250 mg/100 ml. After a month she was transferred to a general medical ward for a cataract operation. She stayed there five months because her eye was slow to clear up and there was delay over her new glasses. She behaved rationally most of the time, but occasionally complained that she was being watched. She was discharged for convalescence on June 7, 1946.

Two months later she wrote to the ward sister complaining that she was under the control of a mysterious man's voice, and on Sept. 7, three months after her discharge, she was readmitted to the mental observation wards complaining that this man's voice was talking to her all the time and controlling her actions. On readmission her blood cholesterol was 276 mg/100 ml and her basal metabolic rate was —25 per cent. She did not look frankly myxoedematous. Treatment with 2 gr (0·13 g) of thyroid thrice daily brought her blood cholesterol down to 150 mg in three weeks, but there was no corresponding mental improvement, and on Nov. 15 she was certified and transferred to Shenley Mental Hospital.

Case 3

A housewife aged 50 was admitted on an authorised officer's order on Aug. 16, 1946, with delusions and hallucinations. For three months she had been getting increasingly dull mentally, gaining weight, and becoming constipated. For one week she had expressed ideas of persecution, saying that many people were plotting against her. She also believed that she was ridden with incurable diseases, and that she might infect everyone. She was continuously terrified by strange voices and strange faces.

On examination she was hallucinated, deluded, and persecuted as described above. She told the doctor estimating her basal metabolic rate that he was in danger of catching typhoid, syphilis, and cancer if he came near her. She was slow in her responses and very depressed and disorientated. Her appearance was typically myxoedematous.

The 'strawberry and cream' complexion was well marked and the palpebral tissues were narrowed by compression with myxoedematous tissue. The voice was thick, grating, and nasal. Her hair was coarse but profuse, and her skin thick and scaly. The pulse was 76, cholesterol 428 mg/100 ml, basal metabolic rate −25 per cent, and blood pressure 155/110.

Progress. On Aug. 23 she was given 1 gr of thyroid twice daily, the dose being gradually increased to 2 gr three times a day on Sept. 12. There was a very rapid improvement in both her appearance and her mental state. Within 10 days she was much more alert, and as well as being free from delusions and hallucinations she had insight—realising the foolishness and asburdity of her previous ideas. Her cholesterol had come down from 428 to 253 mg/100 ml, but her basal metabolic rate was still −22 per cent. When she had become clear-minded she told us that she had been in Redhill Hospital two years before, where she had been given some tablets which made her feel brighter and thinner. (Inquires at Redhill disclosed that she had been an in-patient there from Nov. 12 to 21, 1944, suffering from myxoedema, and had rapidly improved with 2 gr of thyroid thrice daily. After discharge her practitioner had discontinued the treatment.) Her mental and physical improvement continued rapidly; she was discharged to the out-patient department a month after admission and continues to attend there in very good health.

Case 4

A housewife aged 73 was admitted on Dec. 23, 1946, as a case of 'bronchitis'. On admission she was quite confused, could give no coherent history at all, and was obviously grossly demented. She showed no evidence of actual delusions or hallucinations. A history was not available.

On examination she was stuporous and slow, had occasional bouts of restlessness, and was grossly demented. She was flagrantly myxoedematous. Her whole body was spongy with myxomatous tissue, which was especially striking around the eyes and above the clavicles, and which distended the lower lip. Her voice was thick, croaking, and nasal in character. She breathed with a thick, stertorous snorting sound. Her hair was scanty. Her colouring was of the classical pink-and-white variety. The pulse was 60 and the cholesterol 166 mg/100 ml (a surprisingly low figure). She was too ill for the basal metabolic rate to be taken. The blood pressure was not recordable.

Progress. She was given thyroid, $\frac{1}{2}$ gr (32 mg) thrice daily, on admission, increased two days later to 1 gr thrice daily. Five days after admission she became more restless and confused, disturbing the rest of the ward. The next day she suddenly collapsed, became cyanosed and unconscious, with bubbling respiration, and died shortly afterwards.

Post-mortem examination showed a small thyroid (13 g) with normal macroscopic appearance, but microscopically showing marked fibrosis, atrophy of the lobules, and almost complete absence of colloid, with replacement by lymphoid tissue. The heart (480 g) showed myocardial hypertrophy of both ventricles, with gross dilatation of the right heart. The lungs showed congestion and oedema, with some pus in the trachea and main bronchi.

Case 5

A housewife aged 72 was admitted to a medical ward on Jan. 6, 1947, having collapsed unconscious five hours before admission. She was just recovering consciousness when admitted. For two years she had been putting on weight and feeling tired, drowsy, and unusually cold. She had also noticed her hair falling out and her hearing getting worse. On the day of admission she collapsed unconscious, with snoring respiration.

On admission she was slow and inclined to ramble, though rational and orientated. Two days later she became completely confused, noisy, and irrational. She had no idea where she was, and repeatedly said, 'I must go home and look after my son'. The other patients were so much upset by her restless mutterings that she had to be transferred to the mental observation ward.

She had a typical myxoedematous appearance and colouring. The oedema of her eyelids was particularly pronounced; her left eye, blind and atrophied after an old injury, was completely occluded by myxomatous swelling, and appeared visible only after thyroid treatment. The pulse was 70, cholesterol 320 mg/100 ml, blood pressure 220/120. The basal metabolic rate could not be taken.

Progress. She was started on thyroid, $\frac{1}{4}$ gr (16 mg) twice daily on Jan. 7, increased gradually to 2 gr three times a day on Jan. 18. There was rapid improvement in both her mental confusion and her myxoedematous appearance. The blood cholesterol came down from 320 to 130 mg in a fortnight. She became mentally quite clear within a week and was transferred back to a general medical ward. After a month she was discharged perfectly clear mentally, and physically free from any signs of myxoedema. She continues to attend the out-patient department for further supplies of thyroid.

Case 6

A woman of no occupation aged 67 was admitted on an authorised officer's order on Feb. 4, 1947, demented, confused, and disorientated. Her landlady said that for three years she had been 'going senile'. She needed reminding about everything and took two hours to get ready to go out. Once a fine pianist, she had lost all interest in music. During the week before admission she had attacks of screaming and violence, set her nightgown on fire, and became generally quite unmanageable.

On examination she was so slow and lethargic that she would fall asleep while being interviewed; she was quite confused and out of touch with the world, and was unable to give any account of herself whatever.

Physically, she gave an immediate impression of myxoedema. She had the pink-and-white complexion; coarse, thick skin and hair; slow, deep, nasally obstructed voice; and scanty eyebrows. The pulse was 66, cholesterol 300 mg/100 mg, blood pressure 156/100. The basal metabolic rate could not be taken.

Progress. On Feb. 4 she was started on ¼ gr of thyroid three times a day, gradually increasing to 2 gr three times a day on Feb. 24. There was a rapid improvement in both her appearance and her sanity. Within a fortnight she was fit for a general ward and within a month was discharged. Her blood cholesterol had fallen from 300 mg/100 ml on admission to 125 mg on discharge. She attends her own doctor for further supplies of thyroid, and is in good physical and mental health.

Case 7

A housewife aged 54 was admitted on an authorised officer's order on March 13, 1947, with alternating excitement and depression, and ideas of persecution. For one year she had been getting slow and dull, and losing interest in herself and the house. A marked increase in weight and coarsening of her features had been noticed by her relatives. Her sister-in-law said: 'When I was in a hospital once I saw somebody with 'lack of thyroid', and she looked just like my sister-in-law does now, so I've always thought she must have the same illness. I tried to persuade her to see a doctor, but she wouldn't go'. For a week before admission she had been alternately excitable and depressed, at times behaving violently. She had told her relatives that various people were plotting to do her harm and she had accused her husband of attempting to poison her.

On examination she was depressed, confused, and persecuted. She babbled disconnected nonsense about fire-and-water vengeance and the Bible, and could not give any rational account of herself. Whenever anyone approached her bed she would cling to their hands, begging for mercy. She showed the appearance of advanced myxoedema. Her face was bloated and she had a butterfly-shaped flush on the nose and cheeks. Her skin was thick and rough. Her voice was thick and hoarse, with a nasally obstructed quality. The lips were noticeably thickened. The scalp hair was fine and plentiful, the eyebrows sparse. The pulse was 60, blood cholesterol 364 mg/100 ml, blood pressure 180/110. The basal metabolic rate was impossible to take.

Progress. On March 14 she was given thyroid, ½ gr three times a day, increased gradually to 2 gr three times a day on March 20. At first there was rapid improvement in her physical appearance, with no corresponding mental change. Her blood cholesterol came down from 364 to 226 mg in three weeks. Her depression, persecutory ideas, and general unruliness continued for five weeks, and, if anything, thyroid treatment seemed to lend more vigour to her misbehaviour—she was a sore trial to everyone. Then, suddenly, on April 21 she became rational, cheerful, and orientated, with almost complete amnesia over her period of confusion. For a further week she had occasional bouts of weeping, after which time she remained cheerful, happy, and perfectly normal both mentally and physically. She continues to attend as an out-patient, in vigorous health.

Case 8

A housewife aged 62 was admitted on an authorised officer's order on May 15, 1947, with systematised delusions. Her sister said she had always been rather simple. For one month she had become restless and deluded. She wandered round the house, packing up her belongings and saying that she was going to the seaside. She maintained solidly that she and her husband had a house at Leigh-on-Sea, and that there she must go (there was no truth in this whatever).

On examination she was quiet and co-operative, but incapable of giving a history and unwilling to submit to a basal-metabolic-rate test. She insisted that her husband was living somewhere in the hospital. Throughout her stay she persisted with the delusion that she had a house at Leigh-on-Sea. She was a shrivelled little old lady, not very myxoedematous to look at. She had wrinkled dry skin of yellowish parchment colour. There was gross alopecia. Her voice was high, with a grating, scrannel character, but was not the usual myxoedematous voice. There were no other signs. The pulse was 80 and the blood cholesterol 400 mg/100 ml; the basal metabolic rate was impossible to obtain, and the blood pressure was not taken.

Progress. She was started on thyroid, 1 gr thrice daily, gradually increasing to 3 gr thrice daily. There was a steady change in her appearance and within six weeks she looked 15 years younger. The blood cholesterol came down steadily thus: May 15, 400 mg/100 ml; May 25, 349 mg; June 4, 287 mg; June 24, 218 mg. It was most disappointing that there was no corresponding mental improvement. She persisted in her delusions with, if anything, more conviction and vigour than before. I waited two months to see if the psychosis would clear, and then, on July 9, transferred her to Shenley Mental Hospital as a certified patient.

Case 9

A housewife aged 56 was transferred from Hillingdon Hospital on May 28, 1947, for investigation as a case of suspected cerebral tumour or subdural haematoma. She had already been diagnosed as suffering from myxoedema.

One year previously she had been admitted to Hillingdon as a possible case of Alzheimer's disease. At that time she complained of six months' chronic head pains, depression, loss of concentration, and attacks of palpitations and panic. She was said to have been a lively person and good company before the illness, but had become so dull she could not work out ordinary money problems. On that admission nothing abnormal was noted, though she was observed to have an unusually deep, husky voice. She was discharged slightly improved after three weeks.

She was readmitted to Hillingdon on April 26, 1947, suffering from right thoracic herpes zoster and mental symptoms. She was completely confused, and was comatose most of the time but occasionally restless and violent.

Physical examination revealed an appearance of myxoedema. She had a sallow thick skin, a husky deep voice, and scanty eyebrows. There were oedematous pads above both clavicles and she was very deaf. The pulse was 90, basal metabolic rate −27 per cent, blood cholesterol 333 mg/100 ml, blood pressure 200/120.

She was treated with thyroid, 3 gr daily for 14 days, reduced after three weeks to 1 gr daily. During a bout of restlessness on May 4 she fell out of bed and sustained a large haematoma in the centre of the forehead. Because of increased mental confusion and a suggestion of early papilloedema she was transferred on May 28 to the Central Middlesex County Hospital under Mr T. I. G. James for neurosurgical investigation.

On admission she was still mildly myxoedematous in appearance. The blood cholesterol was 272 mg/100 ml, the pulse 75. No abnormal neurological findings were made. The encephalogram was normal. It was therefore considered that her mental symptoms were myxoedematous. The dose of thyroid was increased to 2 gr three times a day. She was transferred back to Hillingdon on June 16, where, with further thyroid treatment, her mental condition gradually became normal and she was discharged for convalescence on July 11.

Case 10

A housewife aged 64 was admitted to Hillingdon Hospital under Dr C. G. Barnes on Feb. 21, 1948, as a case of 'chronic heart and renal back pressure'. Dr Barnes kindly asked me to see her on Feb. 27. Her husband stated that for one year her face had been getting puffy, for six months she had swelling of the legs and difficulty in walking, and for one month she had been bedridden. A week before admission she became quite confused and delirious, and remained so until the day of admission, when she became comatose.

On examination she was semicomatose, with shallow respiration and a slow pulse. Her eyes were completely closed by oedema and could not be opened. Her face was typical of an unusually advanced degree of myxoedema, with a striking yellow skin and malar flush. She was partially bald, her eyebrows were scanty, and her eyelashes almost completely absent. The pulse was 60 and blood cholesterol 486 mg/100 ml; the basal metabolic rate was impossible to obtain.

She was given 10 gr (0·65 g) of thyroid the same day, as Dr Barnes feared that otherwise she would suffocate or die from bronchopneumonia.

Progress. During the next two days she became more deeply comatose, but on the third day she became conscious and her eyes were visible. She was restless and hallucinated. She complained that 'Joe the Shadow' was trying to do her harm and that people were watching her. She shouted about pictures on the ceiling and told me that she heard pianos and singing. She remained maniacal and hallucinated for over fortnight. She was given 1 gr of thyroid daily and her myxoedematous appearance and her mental state steadily improved. After two months she looked nearly normal and her confusion had almost gone. On April 1 the basal metabolic rate was +2 per cent and the blood cholesterol had come down from 486 to 314 mg/100 ml. She was discharged home on April 1, fit and rational.

Case 11

A housewife aged 53 was admitted on Feb. 23, 1948, complaining of tiredness and undue gain in weight. Fifteen months previously she had had a cholecystectomy for gall-stones. For six months she had felt weary and had gained much weight. She complained of chronic catarrh and said her voice had become coarse and her skin rough.

On examination she was slow and rather drowsy, but appeared rational until a week later, when she showed delusions of persecution. She said she had been accused of wrongdoing by the hospital staff and believed that she had been admitted for punishment. She told me that all the other patients were whispering to each other, saying unpleasant things about her. She had to be transferred to the mental observation ward on March 8, as her paranoid ideas were getting worse.

Physically she had the typical appearance of fully developed myxoedema. Her features were swollen, the normal facial creases being ironed out by the swelling. Her face was a waxy yellow colour. Her eyebrows were scanty, her skin dry, her speech thick and indicative of nasal obstruction. Her blood cholesterol was higher that that of other cases in this series—610 mg/100 ml. The palms of her hands had yellow bands 0·25 cm wide, corresponding to the creases. These were cholesterol deposits, the same colour as the xanthelasma of hypercholesterolaemia, and they steadily faded during the next two months as the blood cholesterol fell with treatment. (The high blood cholesterol might also have contributed to the gall-stones from which she had suffered.) The pulse was 75 and the basal metabolic rate −8 per cent; the blood pressure was 155/90.

Progress. She was given thyroid, 1 gr three times a day, on Feb. 27, increasing gradually to 2 gr four times daily on March 19. At first her mental symptoms grew worse, while her appearance improved. By March 11 she had some insight into her previous irrationality, and by March 13 she was mentally normal, remaining so until her discharge to the out-patient department on March 25.

Case 12

This patient was a physician aged 33. During a lecture on myxoedema to some doctors taking a membership course in 1946 I described the mental changes I had so often encountered, and mentioned that ideas of persecution were common. At the end of the lecture the patient came up to me and explained that he was a known case of myxoedema and gave the following history.

In 1941, while with the Army in West Africa, he felt tired, dull, and slow. At the same time he developed ideas of persecution. These symptoms continued unchanged until February, 1942, when he was diagnosed as a definite case of myxoedema and ordered thyroid, 3 gr daily. The persecutional ideas disappeared completely in a short time and he felt a striking improvement in his feeling of well-being. In 1945, while in Italy, he began to wonder if it was really necessary to go on taking thyroid, so he stopped. The mental symptoms crept insidiously back and there was a falling off in his general efficiency. Eventually he found himself unwilling to go into the mess with his fellow officers because he believed they were talking about him, criticising him, and plotting against him in some way. He resumed thyroid treatment again, and his persecutional ideas once more disappeared rapidly. Since that time he has continued to take thyroid in various doses, at present being stabilised on 6 gr daily and remaining mentally and physically quite well.

When I saw him his appearance seemed normal (I did not examine him professionally), but he had some malar flush and his voice was a little lower and slower than the average. He had not previously mentioned his mental symptoms to anyone lest they indicated a true psychotic tendency, but on learning that they were merely a part of his hypothyroid symptoms he was much relieved and quite pleased to admit them. He has very kindly agreed to my publishing these details about his case.

Case 13

A housewife aged 62 was admitted on March 18, 1949, on an authorised officer's order, suffering from confusion and dementia. Her husband said that for about four years she had been increasingly slow in mind and body. She often complained of coldness and deafness, and became very forgetful. She 'snored something awful'. A week before admission she became unable to walk. Her voice was so thick no one could understand her. She stared blankly about her and seemed unaware of what was going on.

On examination she was mentally in a state of hibernation, and an unintelligible croaking monosyllable was the only reply to questioning. Her mind seemed to have stopped functioning rather than to have become disordered.

Physically she was the grossest case of myxoedema in the series. Her face was bloated and misshapen, with great wine-coloured patches on a dusky yellow background. She was dirty, unkempt, and partially bald. Her skin was as cold and rough as a lizard's. Her pulse was 48, temperature 97°F (36·1°C), respirations 16.

Progress. She died early the next morning before any investigations had been done, so the cholesterol value, the basal metabolic rate, and the blood pressure were not known. A coroner's inquest reported death from acute heart failure due to myxoedema. The thyroid was completely replaced by white fibrous tissue, but was otherwise normal in size and shape. The heart was dilated and hypertrophied, and there was a pericardial effusion.

Case 14

A housewife aged 53 was admitted on an authorised officer's order on March 29, 1949, suffering from hallucinations and delusions of persecution. For three months she had complained that she was being persecuted by the people in the flat above her. She tried to persuade her husband that they were spying upon her down a ventilator pipe. She heard voices saying unpleasant things to her, particularly at night. She also began to snore excessively, and because of this she went to the out-patient ENT department of a large voluntary hospital. Her delusions and hallucinations were so flagrant, however, that she was immediately referred to the psychiatric department. The senior psychiatrist then referred her to the authorising officer as a case of paranoid psychosis.

When deliberately questioned she admitted that for two years her hair had been coming out, her voice had been getting deeper, and her skin had become dry. She said she felt so cold and sleepy she wanted to curl up and go into a long, long sleep.

On examination she was found to be persecuted, deluded, and hallucinated, and she complained of the voices pestering her continually. She was typically though not grossly myxoedematous. The skin of her face was yellow with a malar flush, the palpebral fissures were narrow, and the eyebrows scanty. Her voice was thick and croaking. Her pulse was 68, cholesterol 250 mg/100 ml, blood pressure 130/90. The basal metabolic rate was impossible to take (she thought she was being gassed).

Progress. She was started on thyroid, ½ gr thrice daily, increased five days later to 1 gr thrice daily. Within a fortnight there was an obvious facial change and she began to have insight into her hallucinations—admitting they were not real voices though she still heard them. After three weeks the cholesterol had come down from 250 to 120 mg, the hallucinations had stopped, and she said, 'I feel different, I see things different, and my husband says I look younger. I talk different; I've lost that deep tone and seem to speak lighter'. She was discharged a month after admission and continues to attend as an out-patient in normal physical and mental health. Soon after discharge, when she went to her grocer he said to her: 'Are you a relation of the Mrs —— who used to come in here and went to hospital?' He had completely failed to recognise her.

DISCUSSION

It is hoped that publication of these fourteen case reports may call attention to the very important fact that myxoedema causes psychosis. If one observer can encounter this number in four years it must mean that there are many others. Possibly there are many cases in mental hospitals which have not been diagnosed. If the diagnosis is borne in mind by psychiatrists a number of otherwise hopeless psychoses may be cured, and the awareness of an organic cause for one psychosis may lead to the discovery of physical causes for others which are at present dismissed as of psychological or idiopathic origin.

How to Diagnose Myxoedema

As this paper has stressed the importance of early diagnosis and treatment of myxoedema, it seems logical to summarise the methods by which a diagnosis can be made, especially as these case records show that in no instance was the diagnosis made before the patient came to hospital.

The history gives little help in making a diagnosis, though it greatly helps in confirming it once the condition is suspected; that is because the symptoms are admitted rather than complained of; they are dismissed by the patient as minor nuisances rather than exhibited as major complaints, and are therefore usually elicited only when the appropriate questions are asked. The mental slowness of the illness itself smothers self-criticism, and so changes may pass unnoticed by the patient while friends and relations observe them. In fact, you get no history of myxoedema if you are not thinking of myxoedema when you take that history.

The following symptoms are common: general tiredness, gain in weight, vague aching pains in the legs, poor memory, constipation, deafness, falling out of hair, dry skin, always feeling cold. All these symptoms commonly occur in non-myxoedematous people and not one of them is constant in myxoedema. Change in the facial appearance, alteration in the voice, and snoring are usually noticed by relatives rather than by the patient.

The only way to ascertain what a case of myxoedema looks like is to see one. No amount of description can convey the unmistakable impression of a well-developed case. Photographs are more helpful than words, but give no idea of the characteristic colouring and voice. Here is a description of an advanced case.

Nearly all cases occur in women. The features look bloated and the normal contours of the face are smoothed away, just as the wrinkles of a balloon disappear when it is blown out. Oedema collects in the lips, broadening them, and around the eyes, forming little bags of flesh beneath them. When, after treatment, the swelling round the eyes subsides there is sometimes revealed a slight exophthalmos, possibly due to the anterior pituitary's efforts to flog an inactive thyroid. The colour is yellowish and waxy, with a contrasting burgundy-coloured flush over the malar bones. The hair is dry and scanty, the receding hair margin leaves a wide forehead, and there may be partial baldness. The eyebrows are sparse, and sometimes the lashes too. The classical loss of hair over the outer third of the eyebrows is an unreliable sign, because so many normal people show this deficiency.

The voice is slow and fumbling from the clumsy thickness of the lips and tongue, and the oedematous infiltration of the nasal passages gives it a characteristic nasal quality. It is impossible to imprison the sound in words, but the impression is that of a bad gramophone record of a drowsy, slightly intoxicated person with a bad cold and a plum in the mouth. Snoring (Morehead, 1936), already mentioned as a symptom, may be of arresting intensity, and it is odd that in a discussion on snoring at the Royal Society of Medicine no mention was made of myxoedema as one of its causes.

The description here given is that of an unusually obvious case. The recognition of an early or a mild case is harder but is more satisfying than recognising the self-evident one. Mild cases are probably often missed because the textbook illustrations always picture an unusually gross case and not the moderate cases which are more often encountered. Mistakes are also made through expecting every sign to be present, whereas the average case lacks at least one of the classical features of the illness; for example, Case 3 had luxuriant eyebrows, Case 4 had a low blood cholesterol, Case 8 had no puffiness of the face, Case 9 had a raised pulse, and Case 11 had a normal basal metabolic rate.

Confirmatory Tests

Photographic Test. I consider there is only one infallible confirmatory test for myxoedema. Take a good photograph; then give thyroid for a month or more and take another photograph. The change between the two photographs is clear confirmation of the diagnosis. In many cases where I have not been certain of the diagnosis the change recorded by photographs has been the only unequivocal proof of the answer.

I would like to stress here that only a proportion of myxoedema cases have psychotic changes, and that these remarks on the diagnosis of myxoedema apply to all cases, with or without mental symptoms.

Blood Cholesterol. This is nearly always raised, and, furthermore, descends with thyroid treatment. In ten of these cases the initial blood cholesterol was 300 mg or more per 100 ml, and it usually descended by over 100 mg/100 ml after thyroid treatment. Blood cholesterol estimations are, after photographs, the best confirmatory tests.

Basal Metabolic Rate. From experience with many other cases besides these I have found the basal metabolic rate of little help in diagnosing myxoedema. It is a test which is accepted when it agrees with the physician and disregarded when it does not. I have seen many cases of myxoedema with normal or raised BMR. Further, the presence of mental change or respiratory obstruction may prevent the estimation being done. In only four of the cases described above was the basal metabolic rate taken—Case 2 −26 per cent, Case 3 −25 per cent, Case 9 −27 per cent, Case 11 −8 per cent.

Pulse Rate. The classical bradycardia of the textbook is not common. In four cases the pulse was over 70 and in only two instances was it below 60.

Blood Pressure. In six of these cases there was hypertension (either a systolic pressure above 170 mm Hg or a diastolic pressure above 100 mm Hg).

SUMMARY

Myxoedema is a much commoner cause of psychosis than is usually believed. Treatment with thyroid usually cures the psychosis dramatically. Fourteen cases are described—nine recovered completely, two recovered partially, one showed no change, and two were fatal. There is no specific psychosis, but paranoid ideas are common. A description of myxoedema is given and methods of diagnosing it are reviewed. Photographs before and after thyroid treatment give the best confirmation of the diagnosis.

REFERENCES

Akelaitis, A. J. E. (1936) *J. nerv. ment. Dis.*, **83**, 22.

Buschan, G. (1896) *Uber Myxödem und verwandte Zustände*, p. 60.

Committee of the Clinical Society of London (1888) *Trans. clin. Soc.*, Supplement to vol. 21.

Cronin, A. J. (1937) *The Citadel.* London.

Morehead, D. E. (1936) *Minn. Med.*, **19**, 641.

Ruhberg, G. N. (1936) Ibid., **19**, 637.

Stoll, H. F. (1932) *Ann. intern. Med.*, **6**, 806.

Zondek, H., and Wolfsohn, G. (1944) *Lancet*, **2**, 438.

7

*Aren't I Lucky? I Can Write!**

I can write things which most people can understand, and some people enjoy. How arrogant that sounds, but I am not writing an article on how modest I am, I am writing about being able to write.

People often say to me 'Oh, you're lucky! You can write! What a lot of pleasure you must get out of it.'

I admit that I can write, but I am not particularly proud of it, nor do I get a great deal of pleasure from it. Then why on earth do I write?

I usually write because I have been asked to do so; that is why I write now. If I said I was too busy to write for this magazine, how unhelpful and superior you would think me. You know perfectly well that it is easy for me. I need only sit in an armchair with some foolscap on my knee, scrawl a few words, and say to my secretary, 'Oh Sally, type this out and pop it along to the Nursing Staff magazine; I hear they want me to write something for them.' Or I could loll in my office chair with a cigarette in one hand and a microphone in the other and chat into the mike for a minute or two. Then put my feet on the desk and have a little nap while Sally typed it from the tape machine. I would give the proofs to a student or houseman to correct. Yet, for this trifling effort, I should be thanked profusely. 'How very kind of you to write for us. I know how busy you are. It really is very good of you.'

My dear reader, I know how different you are. You would never give yourself airs like me. Had you the gift of writing, you would gladly oblige all the people who wanted you to write for them, just as if you had the good fortune to own a private aeroplane you would always be giving lifts to your friends. You don't even have to pay

* Written for the Central Middlesex Hospital Nurses' Magazine in September 1961.

for petrol or licence as you do with an aeroplane; writing costs absolutely nothing. How you must wish you had this priceless gift. You would get so much fun out of it, and a nice little private income as well. You would never adopt a cynical, disillusioned attitude like that crusty old fellow Asher, would you? Of course not. You would be pleased with your gift, but in a nice modest way; 'Oh well, I'm lucky; I just happen to be able to write. I'd love to help you. What sort of thing would you like?' Charming!

My dear, warm-hearted reader, your unselfish and generous attitude deserves the highest praise; but . . .

Have you ever tried writing?

No? I thought you could not have done. It is so laborious and tedious that authors often despair of getting their ideas on to paper at all. It is hard enough to find ideas worth writing, but harder still to put them into words worth reading. Some ideas seem admirable, flitting through the semi-darkness of your mind, but once they are pinioned on paper, you see they are trivial valueless specimens.

Let us imagine you have a few ideas. You try to write them down, but the first version of what you want to say sounds so clumsy and puts your ideas so badly, you throw it away and start again. You may work for a whole evening and finish with a full waste-paper basket and only one worth-while paragraph surviving. When you have put down what you wanted to say, you are only beginning. Then you start working on it. You cross out many words that you can do without. You change words which sound wrong for others which sound right. The article begins to look a little better, but the parts you have altered do not join up properly, and you notice that many sentences might read better if you turned them the other way round. For example, instead of 'the parts you have altered, do not join up properly' I could have written 'some parts do not join up properly because you have altered them', or 'because of your alterations the proper joining-up of the parts has been lost'. Well, does it matter?

If the different versions sound equally good, it does not matter, but usually there is a lot of difference. Will you agree that 'the proper joining-up of the parts has been lost' sounds clumsy? You can't imagine 'a joining-up' being lost. You could try 'fusion' instead of 'joining-up', but it sounds wrong even though the meaning is right. It is much better to have: 'The parts you have altered do not join up properly'. Do you agree?

'All right', you say, 'but surely it doesn't matter with what you're writing now; this is casual writing, with "don't" instead of "do not", "you're" instead of "you are", etc.; you aren't making an effort to write, you're just talking.'

My dear reader (I hope you don't mind my calling you that, I picked up the habit from Anthony Trollope), if you truly believe I am writing effortlessly, you are paying me a great compliment. To write with apparent ease is what every author wants, but this requires more grinding effort than any non-writer could ever guess.

To return to the MS; when you have juggled with the order of the words and exchanged the most uncomfortable words, your manuscript is in a sorry state. It is written in long-hand (you can juggle words with a pen, but not with a typewriter). Many of the words are changed back again; you realised the first one was better after all. You have shifted whole sentences or paragraphs by drawing a ring round them with an arrow leading to a better place. When you found a better place still, you crossed out the first arrow, but with a wiggly line so it wouldn't look like another arrow, or with lots of little lines like railway sleepers. You have drawn some odd pictures while you were thinking, and jotted down a few telephone numbers, and the time your wife asked you to light the oven. There are brown rings where you stood a cup of tea. You can hardly read the manuscript and you could not ask any secretary to type it for you. Why not go to bed? It is long after midnight. No. You are so keen to get it over, you will do it now so it will be all ready for typing tomorrow. You vow you will not change one word, you will only copy what you have already decided.

As you are copying it you think of a much better way of writing one sentence. You cannot resist the change. As you put it down, you find you have forgotten how it went. Or you remember that you tried it that way several days ago, and 'it won't come out'. You have some strong tea, determined to finish tonight. If you are typing it, when you finish one of the longest and most difficult pages you find the carbon was the wrong way round and there is a shameful blue 'looking-glass' version on the back of your top copy. (Anyway, a carbon copy is no use at this stage.)

Finally, you go to bed, leaving everything in a mess but with a manuscript fit to give an intelligent and tolerant secretary. You take it to her next day, not daring to look at it in case you start making alterations again. You tell her about the passage you have crossed out on page 2 which you want to have back again after all, and the bit on page 1 which is to be inserted where you put the arrow on page 5. You ask for treble spacing, because there will still be many alterations to make.

When it comes back, the typewritten words seem to read differently from the same words in longhand. You can see obvious flaws you never noticed before, and you notice some sentences that could be

written far more clearly in a quarter of the words. Why in heaven's name did you write: 'In regard to one's fondness for animals, there are, naturally, individual preferences depending on a number of factors, but personally, despite the understandable and widespread popularity of dogs among animal lovers, I have, myself, for a number of years, regarded cats with a considerable degree of affection'?

It only means 'Some people like dogs, but I like cats'. Blast!

Of course, the first sentence had a certain something. It sounds more like print than the other, the kind of thing you might read anywhere. Not particularly interesting, but it sounds as if it meant a bit more. You couldn't write 'Some people like dogs but I like cats'. It sounds so silly.

Then you are attacked with questions by that bogy which clergymen used to call 'the small inner voice'. 'Come off it', says the s.i.v., 'That is a silly remark. Is it any less silly when stuffed with bosh like "depending on a number of factors" which means nothing whatever?' Eventually the s.i.v. forces you to realise that the silliness is far less noticeable when disguised by stuffing, but just as silly. Sadly, you scrap the whole outfit: cats, dogs, a number of factors and all. Oh blast!

I will not describe the other stages an article goes through: You put it away for a week or two and then you see many faults you missed before. You try it on a critical and literate friend who finds many more. The editor of the journal who prints it (if it is good enough for them to print it) may annihilate hours of work with a few seconds of blue-pencilled butchery. The article is much better when cut by a third, but the author's wound smarts for a long time. The proof reading is very important. Delegate it of course; but do it yourself as well. Your friends notice errors you missed and vice versa. If the article is any good your friends get interested in what you have written instead of looking for slips. It is worth taking trouble. Did you notice those poor daffodils in a recent issue of this journal? They were 'crowing' beneath the trees. How gravely they lost dignity from the shrill polophonic squawking which that word conjured up. Had they been left 'growing', or even 'crowding' beneath the trees, they could have kept a dignified silence.

At the end of this article I give a few facts about its preparation, not to impress you with the trouble I have taken but to illustrate the points I have made. I have taken trouble only because I am incapable of producing anything worth reading except by a laborious process. I am not thinking of you while I write. I am thinking only of myself and whether I am satisfied with what I have written. When, at rare moments, I did think of you, it was not with any tenderness.

'Will anybody read this magazine?' 'Not many nurses if they have to pay for it!' 'They probably read nothing but Peter Cheyney, Agatha Christie and Ruby M. Ayres.' 'Do they get the magazine free from the Management Committee?' (They love distributing any kind of cyclostyled or printed document.) 'If so, the magazine may come in useful to jam a rattling window.' 'What a waste of time taking all this trouble.'

I expect no thanks, and I deserve none. The best I can hope for is, 'Well, it's not bad, but it wasn't worth all that trouble.' I agree with you.

I am cheered to learn that many authors have similar difficulties. I suspect that anyone who writes acceptable prose takes a good deal of trouble. Somerset Maugham admits that he does, and he records his surprise that Colette, whose effortless style he much admired, wrote and re-wrote every page countless times. If Maugham and Colette find writing as difficult as I do, it has at least brought them fame and fortune; to me it has brought neither. I am not a particularly good author, and I claim no more than what I said on the first page, 'I can write things which most people can understand, and some people enjoy'. I hope that most people have understood this, and that some people have enjoyed it. Writing is done more by toil than by gift. Is it worth it? I don't really think it is. Then why do I write? Honestly I don't know; but 'this is where I came in'. Aren't I lucky? I can write! Goodbye.

BALANCE SHEET

I kept no accounts, so this is not accurate. I only thought of including these figures when the article was almost complete.

Expenditure

Thinking of Ideas. Not strenuous work. Done at odd moments, driving to hospital, painting the bathroom, or while lying in bed.	3 to 4 hours
Writing Headings. Putting down ideas, just rough outlines without sentences. Arranging them in order.	2 to 3 hours
Writing first draft. I have estimated four to five evenings at 2 to 3 hours actual work per evening. I work fitfully. I break to empty the waste-paper basket into the dustbin, and am diverted to do some photography when I reach the basement, or to play a duet with one of my children. Then mugs of strong tea and resume work. I rarely go to bed before 2 a.m., not all hard work; mostly pottering.	12 hours (approx)
Amending and re-writing. I hardly dare estimate. I wrote the whole thing in longhand three times, each incorporating alterations in its predecessor. I typed it out in full twice. Then my secretary typed it. Since then I have typed it out twice more. Each version was altered and re-altered till unreadable.	10 to 20 hours, it is impossible to total this; one keeps leaving it and going back to it.

8

*The Medical Education of the Patient and the Public**

I see this discussion has been announced in the Journal as The Medical Education of the Patient, but when I was asked to speak, it was on the Patient *and* the Public, and as I only noticed the difference last night, it is too late to change. Anyway, I was told, when I was asked to speak on this subject, that it was on account of my provocative powers, so the fact that my talk has been prepared on the wrong subject should give me a certain advantage in provoking you.

I shall deal with this subject under three headings: First, should the public have any medical education at all? Secondly, from what sources do they get their medical education at present? Thirdly, what sort of medical education is best for them, and what reforms in their medical education are advisable?

First. Should the public have any medical education at all? Most of us have no idea how our wireless sets work. If they go wrong, we take them to the wireless shop. Should the laity regard their bodies in the same way—as something they take for granted but do not understand; something they take to the body shop (consulting room) when they go wrong.

No! That is impossible, even though we doctors might wish for it. Bodies aren't like wireless sets. They are with us all day. We can't help being interested in them. They tickle. They blush. Sometimes they swell. Hair falls off them. We have to put food into them. Sometimes we scratch them. No reasonable body owner can be expected to go about with one of these remarkable structures without

* A lecture delivered on 20th July 1959 in Edinburgh at the Annual British Medical Association Meeting with the Canadian Medical Association.

becoming a little bit curious about what's going on inside, and how to keep it going properly.

So the public must be given some medical education because they demand it. We would be much happier if they didn't have it, but if we, as doctors don't tell them anything they will invent explanations of their own, or they will ask their grandmother, or they will go and ask the local chemist. They will pick up myths and legends which may be harmful. They have to be told something.

Indirectly, a little knowledge of medicine in the hands of our patients may benefit doctors. It is hard for a salesman to remain honest if his customers have no idea whether his goods are satisfactory or not. Blind, ignorant faith in doctors is not always to their benefit, although we appreciate it highly on the rare occasions we obtain it. Heaven defend us from the kind of patient who comes to us and says, 'I want you to have my 17-keto-steroids estimated, and my serum transaminase done'. How much we prefer the patient who says 'I leave to you, doctor'.

So the answer to the first question, should the Public have any medical education at all, is: 'Yes, but not much.'

Next, I pass to the question: 'What sort of medical education are our patients and our public getting today?'

Let us consider the sources, other than casual conversation, by which they get it. First, there is school, but except when Biology is taken as a special subject, there is little teaching of elementary physiology. Most people leave school with little idea of how their bodies work, but I doubt if that matters much because bodies, like wireless sets and cars, often seem to do better if you leave them alone, and don't take any interest in what is going on inside. Nevertheless, a general idea of how the heart and lungs perform their duties, and a notion of the processes of digestion and metabolism makes an interesting addition to general knowledge. I was looking at the material my daughter of thirteen is studying at the P.N.E.U. school she attends, and was surprised to see the advanced standard of the syllabus—haemoglobin and its functions, the metabolism of protein and its breakdown into amino acids, and so on. The different chambers of the heart and their functions, etc.

Then there are medical encyclopaedias. Most of these seem to me to do more harm than good. A nervous or suggestible patient may look through all the diseases and try to diagnose his own symptoms. The other danger is that a patient learns the name of his own illness, looks it up and finds a very gloomy outlook and a host of terrifying complications.

Next, we have newspapers and magazines, which provide a very large proportion of the medical education our patients receive. The medical correspondents of the better papers are very skilled, and their standards are very high, but I am uncertain if their writings are always understood. Some of them are so fully set out, and so lavishly illustrated (especially American magazines) that they are virtually medical textbooks. Some years ago there was a cartoon in the *New Yorker* which showed a surgeon in the middle of an operation turning to his registrar who was reading a copy of *Life* and saying 'What does it say I ought to do next?'

The danger of magazine medicine is that it selects the sensational and eschews the humdrum—the layman does not get a balanced picture of medical work, when every patient is described as having 'doctors and nurses fighting for his life day and night', and new 'wonder drugs' are being rushed by aeroplane to save them. A great error committed by some papers is that in their anxiety for exciting and up-to-date news, they report newly discovered drugs in laudatory terms before their true worth is known. Now it is a strange fact that if a new drug (say for asthma) is prescribed by a doctor the patient thinks little of it, but if he finds it mentioned in the paper, or, more likely still, if his aunt, knowing he has asthma, cuts it out and posts it to him—then his confidence in the drug is unbounded. 'He won't be happy till he gets it.' In the rare cases where a drug extolled by the papers has some genuine merit, it may cause nothing but discord if the public get to hear of it before it is readily available; then a situation like that in Shaw's *The Doctor's Dilemma* may arise. Penicillin and cortisone both got a vast amount of publicity before they were on the market. Lady Florey told me that a cable from America arrived soon after the discovery of penicillin, asking for a bottle of it to be flown over immediately to save the life of a pet bull-dog (illness unspecified). Papers are wont to pronounce the slightest pharmaceutical advance as a 'Wonder Drug', and the combination of a sensational press and a credulous public leads to desperate attempts to get hold of it. The wholly praiseworthy instinct to make any sacrifice for our nearest and dearest, makes a patient's relatives feel that the more unobtainable a drug is, the greater must be the efforts made to obtain it. So we should ask the Press not to praise drugs till their merit is undoubted and their availability assured.

A popular type of medical education provided by many magazines and newspapers is a column answering questions on health matters posed by patients. This feature is often presided over by a pseudonymous nurse or sister: 'Send your health problem is confidence to Nurse Nincompoop for free advice'.

Many people seem quite happy to have their most intimate problems broadcast in this way. I expect it satisfies the universal urge to appear in print. If you can't get a letter or an article published, at least you can publish the behaviour of your intestines. Even though the answers given in such columns are usually quite sound, the medical benefit to readers is questionable. Nevertheless, the pleasure they impart to others is immense. Other people's troubles are very cheering. 'Poor thing! How fearful!' they mutter as they avidly pore over the dreadful symptoms. Indirectly, these questions and answers are helpful to doctors in preventing them from thinking too highly of themselves: I mean, when they read this kind of thing. 'My doctor says I have got pernicious anaemia and that I will have to be given regular injections for the rest of my life. Is this really true, and what do you advise me to do about it?'

Magazines and papers often provide a weekly feature written by a doctor. All magazine doctors (whether qualified or not) are 'Eminent Harley Street Specialists'. They usually write a series such as 'Confidences of a Consulting Room', or 'Secrets of a Specialist'. Some of them are clearly written by men of wisdom and experience while others are rather second rate. Talking of the second rate, I wish to mention the influence of certain news items, not designed to provide medical education but written by lay reporters among the general news: It is this kind of report:

'Teresa Teardrop, a little crippled girl with pleading eyes, has lain paralysed for seven long years in a picturesque cottage at Little Sobbing-on-the-Sleeve. But now she is going to have the chance of her life. She is off to London to see the great Harley Street Specialist, Sir Bernard Bogus. For months, all the villagers at Sobbing-on-the-Sleeve have been putting their pennies together, and little Teresa is trying to sell her pet kitten to raise money, but at last the necessary two hundred guineas has been found, and a brave little figure clasping her dolly was whisked off to London this morning with her blue eyes full of happiness. Since the *Sunday Slop* published her picture last week, *Sunday Slop* readers have paid for her Mummy and Daddy to go with her.'

People who read stuff like that are capable of believing anything, and so the idea is established that people in England can be left lying paralysed for years, because there is not enough money available to give them the treatment they need. Whether we approve or disapprove of our National Health Service there is no doubt that things like that do not happen in England today, although Americans would love to believe that they do.

Now I would like to say a word or two about popular psychiatry as purveyed by newspapers, television and stage. It is a special kind of psychiatry which the layman wants to believe, and which is therefore obligingly produced for him. It is based on three rather dubious assumptions—

1. That for every psychiatric case there is one buried cause, hidden deep in the subconscious mind like a festering splinter (it is probably something indecent), and once this is dug out, all will be well. You may remember that in Noel Coward's *Blithe Spirit* the hero, when psychoanalysis was suggested, said: 'I refuse to go through months of expensive humiliation to find out that at the age of three I was desperately in love with my rocking horse.'

2. That if poking around in the murky salacity of the subconscious does not reveal the cause of the trouble, then scientific testing of the mind by the electroencephalogram and the Rorsach's test will reveal the cause without fail.

3. That all badly behaved children would be little angels if only their psychiatric problems were properly understood. If your son is always setting the house on fire, you must be patient because this carries some deep inner meaning. If only you are patient enough, and give him the love and affection he needs, the conflagrations will cease forthwith.

The most welcome effect of the psychiatric education of the public is that there is now a far greater tolerance of mental illness, and much less stigma attached to mental hospitals. A television programme called 'The Hurt Mind' contributed much to this enlightenment, though in my view it left the public with an over-optimistic notion of the results of mental hospital treatment.

The mention of television brings me to those most potent sources of medical education—the wireless and the television. The potency of the television was brought home to me last week when a doctor referred a case of thyrotoxicosis to me for an opinion. He told me in the letter he sent with the patient, that the diagnosis had first been made by the patient's brother who had seen a case in a programme called Emergency Ward 10. What a credit to the actress who portrayed the hyperthyroid rôle so successfully. (I wonder how she managed the exophthalmos?) I treated this particular patient with methyl thiouracil, for I had not seen the programme myself, and I was too shy to ask what the doctors in Emergency Ward 10 had done.

I will say no more about the wireless and television in the medical education of our patients, as I rarely listen to the wireless, and I practically never look at the television except to watch my medical colleagues when they appear upon it. So I turn to the important subject of sex education.

It seems best for this to be given to children as early as they can understand it easily. If the information is given long before puberty, they usually accept it in a disinterested way, being neither shocked nor curious about the matter.

Unfortunately, the information is often given to them in a hurried nervous fashion, confusingly mixed up with religion, bees, and botany.

We doctors, being in day-to-day contact with the facts of life, may find it easy to explain these matters to our children and to advocate that other parents should do likewise, but we should realise it is not always so easy for embarrassed lay parents. Part of the trouble is caused by sheer lack of vocabulary. What a ridiculous thing it is that there is no respectable nomenclature for the urogenital system, except the esoteric jargon of the doctor, or the secret family words which differ in each household. Alas! the short, plain biblical words that Chaucer used are today so heavily tarred by association with smut and obscenity that they can never be spoken between parent and child. I believe this problem is insoluble; a word once contaminated by smut is tarnished for ever. The B.M.A. has had enough trouble over sexual matters already, it would not be fair to ask them to issue a list of approved words; but what a blessing it would be if they could only do so. Then a doctor who wanted to ask a small child if his bowels had moved that day, would not have to stumble through an assortment of childish synonyms, or ask the mother 'What does he call it?' It is purely this ridiculous business of word contamination.

One word, fortunately, has managed to come through unscathed, the word 'mate'. We can say without shame, that animals and human beings mate, and there is no fear of a snigger or a giggle. It is not the meaning, but the associations of a word that matter. By making so many words taboo we increase our embarrassment, stultify our means of communication, and thicken the miasma of prudery and misunderstanding which obscures the subject.

I believe there would be less smut if there were more blunt but respectable words, words kept clean by ventilation and not whispered in taverns with a smirk.

Despite these difficulties, there is a far better understanding of sexual physiology today than there used to be. When I was at school, my housemaster asked one boy who was due to be confirmed, to tell him all that he knew about sex. His reply was 'Please Sir, it's the Latin for "six".' Though this answer revealed a gratifying acquaintance with Classical Language, it suggested that adequate parental instruction had not been given.

Whatever, and whenever sexual education ought to be given it must be realised that sexual physiology and sexual morality are two wholly different subjects. There is no necessity for them to be taught by the same person, or given on the same occasion. There is no doubt or disagreement on the so-called 'facts of life'. (I need not mention them here, as a medical audience I am assuming you know the facts of life.) There they are: indisputable, indubitable, inconvenient and sometimes irrepressible, but they are physiological facts, independent of the moral doctrines attached to them.

Yet on the moral issues, on the question of what is right and what is wrong, there is, and always has been, the widest diversity of opinion, and the greatest measure of disagreement. Nor is there any method of proving what is right and what is wrong. Woe betide anyone not of the Church who pronounces on these matters. My only pronouncement is that if morals are to be taught, they should be taught separately from purely factual biology. Good moralists are not always good biologists, and some good biologists are positively immoral. Schoolboys are taught the chemistry of nitroglycerine without being lectured on the evils of safe-blowing, and knowledge of atomic physics and the electron theory are imparted without considering the ethics of using the atom bomb. In the same way, sexual facts should be administered without any corrective doses of religion being mixed up with them. Morals are a separate matter, of which I have very little knowledge.

A quarter of a century ago when I was a student, doing my midwifery in Whitechapel, ignorance about medical matters was far more widespread than it is today. I can remember delivering a woman who confidently believed her baby would be born through her umbilicus; she was convinced that all babies arrived that way. She would not accept my suggestion that there was a less convenient but more probable route, so we just had to wait to see how things would turn out. As she laboured confidently but misguidedly, I hoped that Sir Eardley Holland had been correct in teaching me to expect it somewhat lower down. It was only about half an hour before the baby was born that she began to lose confidence and called out timidly: 'Doctor, I believe you're going to be right after all'.

Though the matter is of no great moment, and I do not wish to make myself out to be infallible, you may be interested to learn that on that particular occasion, I *was* right.

Today, the level of general knowledge on medical matters is much more advanced, and most, but not all women, know where a baby is likely to arrive. Also the legends of the Stork, or The Gooseberry Bush or the Doctor's Black Bag are all things of the past. All the same, ignorance of the elementary workings and anatomy of the human body is still quite common. Many people would be nonplussed if you asked what part of an animal was the red meat, and surprised to know it was muscle, but I doubt if such ignorance does them any harm.

Now for my third and last question. What reforms in medical education would I like to see? I have only time to mention a few.

In general, I would like to see less attention paid to the sensational, and more to the practical side of medicine. Less about cardiac surgery and more about the prevention of caries by fluorides. On this particular point, I would like the public to realise, that the 'natural' undoctored waters of Malvern which have such a remarkable effect in preventing dental decay, do so by virtue of that same element—fluoride—which, when added by man, they describe as 'compulsory medication' or 'interference with their right to natural pure water'. Would they regard the artificial removal of noxious, but very 'natural' bacteria as interference? In fact I should like the public taught to think rationally and not emotionally.

I would like the public to know that there is no such thing as a chill and that a hot child, sweating after his gym (or her dancing class) can sit in a cool breeze with impunity and joy. I would like the public to realise that, in general, a little of what you fancy does you good. I would like the public to have a rough idea of what is going on inside them, but not enough to make them hypochondriacal. I would like to see a greater limitation of patent medicine advertisements—especially those for purgatives and tranquillisers.

Finally, I would like to see our patients and our public cease their vain strivings after longevity, and to realise that it is better to live for seventy years without fussing, than to achieve the age of eighty with elaborate, painstaking care.

> Life's a pudding full of plums.
> Let us take it as it comes.

9

*Talk, Tact, and Treatment**

I agree with Dr Balint that many doctors select the physical and eschew the psychological factors in their patients' illnesses. I know I am as guilty of this as are most physicians. All the same, we have some excuse, some reason, for being frightened or suspicious of the subject of psychiatry even though we know that psychological factors are important.

Psychiatry seems to me to differ from medicine in having a closer resemblance to religion. Beliefs and dogmas are promulgated by certain masters—Freud, Adler, Jung, and so on—and these ideas are believed more from reverence of their originator than from repeated experimental observation. Secondly, the language of psychiatry, like that of religion, is often esoteric and concerns itself with concepts and abstractions whose exact meaning is less precisely comprehended than are the majority of medical concepts. If for a moment we consider the dynamic formulation of both objective and subjective thought fantasy, then cognitive functions can easily become projected into an integrated but psychically barren wish-fulfilment. That last high-sounding sentence, as I hope you noticed, has no meaning whatever and is pure nonsense; but I wrote it to demonstrate that with the aid of abstract terms it is easy to parade such a brave show of words in front of one's thoughts that it is extremely difficult to see if there is any idea behind them, and it is equally easy to take a small idea and wrap around it such a glittering mantle of language that it can dazzle the unwary into applause. Thus, although much wisdom is written by psychiatrists, the nature of the subject and its language make it hard for the ordinary doctor to distinguish the profound from the profuse.

* From an address to the Medical Section of the British Psychological Society, forming a sequel to the chairman's address by Dr Michael Balint, and published in *The Lancet*, April 1955.

Another difference between psychiatry and medicine is that it is easier to prove the correctness or otherwise of medical ideas. Modern medicine consists to a large extent in debunking the ideas erroneously held by others. We used to treat bloodless limbs by warming them—now we cool them; we used to treat bleeding ulcers by starving them—now we feed them. With psychiatric beliefs experimental proof is much harder. I have recently been reading the views of psychiatrists on the syndrome of depersonalisation. Gordon describes the syndrome as a converted representation of hidden or repressed emotional consciousness by special determination. Perhaps he is right, but Schilder stresses the shift of the libido and its partial concentration on a scrutinising tendency. Here I find myself asking how one can tell if a libido has shifted and what means there are of assessing its scrutinising tendency. Sodger says it may be an attempt to escape psychic castration. Perhaps it may, but for a physician the phenomenon of psychic castration is so much harder to understand than is its physical counterpart. Wittels says it is caused by an unusually large number of phantom figures leaving the ego undecided about which figure should be acknowledged as its representative. As a physician I find myself in complete ignorance as to what is a normal healthy number of phantom figures; would five or six, for instance, be considered excessive?

I have made these few comments to show how much at sea the physician feels when he looks at psychiatric theory, and how bewildered he becomes if he considers how to prove which theory is right.

After this rather lame excuse for the physicians' neglect of psychiatry I will get down to the main body of my subject.

THE DOCTOR AS A DRUG

Dr Balint spoke of the discovery of his seminar that by far the most frequently used drug in general practice was the doctor himself: 'it was not only the medicine in the bottle, or the pills in the box, that mattered but the way the doctor gave them'. Here I am in strong agreement. In the words of a popular song 'It's not what you do, but the way that you do it.' Dr Balint, continuing the analogy of drug and doctor, regrets that textbooks and lecturers teach us the way to use drugs, but not the way to use ourselves. Admittedly the way we deal with our patients, and especially how we talk to them, is about the most important part of our trade; but can it be taught? I doubt it. It can be learnt by experience and to some extent by watching great doctors handling their patients, but it cannot be taught like pharmacology. All the power of tongue and pen, and all the wisdom of textbook and lecture can never teach a doctor the knowledge of when to probe and when to leave alone, when to chide and when to reassure, when to speak and when to keep silent. They are private mysteries with a different solution for every one of the million permutations of personality involved between a doctor and his patient.

I believe the analogy between drugs and doctors is a false one: there is such a great difference between them. Drugs can be standardised and doctors (thank heaven) cannot. If you give a man a pill there are only two things he can do with it: he can swallow it or he can throw it away. If you give a man explanation or advice there are uncountable ways of giving it and even more ways in which it can be taken. Dr Balint tilts at the suggestion that common sense and experience will help the doctor know how to prescribe himself (in fact how to talk to his patients) and says the shallowness of this solution is apparent when it is compared with the careful and detailed instructions with which every new drug is introduced. I think here again the analogy of drug and doctor has been extended too far. On the best way to use drugs there is a certain measure of agreement even though individual patients may react differently, but on the best way to speak to patients there is not. There is some agreement on the correct dose of digitalis for a ten-stone woman fibrillating at 120 beats per minute, but far less agreement on the correct type and dose of conversation for a ten-years-unhappily-married woman vociferating at 120 words per minute. Moreover there are only three or four kinds of digitalis, but innumerable kinds of doctor, and even more kinds of unhappy women.

No: the prescribing of ourselves cannot be taught; it is partly instinctive, partly imitative, and partly acquired by experience. I do, however, consider it to be of enormous importance and I propose to say something on the subject of conversation with patients.

TALKING TO THE DOCTOR

Why does the patient want to talk to his doctor?

First there is the natural desire for companionship. Many people simply want a pleasant chat, but instead of going along to the local public-house for a drink of beer and a chat with the landlord they go along to the local hospital for a drink of medicine and a chat with the doctor. The use of a doctor for this purpose is unnecessary, and a pleasant gossip over a cup of tea with fellow patients is equally satisfying. Indeed one enlightened physician tried the experiment of arranging outpatient sessions where the patients did not see the doctor at all unless they specially asked for him*; this experiment was a great success. Moreover, despite the present high price of tea, a cup of tea is cheaper than a bottle of medicine and far less likely to do any harm.

Another reason why people want to talk to doctors is to get sympathy—they do not want help or advice, they want someone to know how much they are having to bear. A vicar's wife told me once that, much to his distress, parishioners were always wanting to show their ulcerated legs to the vicar. This was done not for spiritual healing, but that he might realise the extent of their sufferings. It is a fact that it is easier to bear a heavy burden if that burden is visible to others. Doctors are told of all sorts of troubles—financial, domestic, or personal—which are beyond their powers to relieve; but all the patient is seeking from them is some remark of the kind: 'I don't know how you put up with it all', or 'I think it's wonderful the way you manage to carry on'. Almost anything can be borne if someone thinks one is wonderful.

Some patients, unlike those I have just mentioned, come for advice. They have problems which are soluble, and they need, not sympathy, but a suggestion as to what is to be done or not to be done. Though it sounds paradoxical to say so, I believe the advice given is often immaterial. The conversation helps the patient to make up his own mind, irrespective of the wisdom of the advice given. Only when he is strongly advised to do *A* does the average person realise how much wiser it would be to do *B*.

Other types of patient come not to see what the doctor has to say but are already firmly decided on what he will say. They come, not for advice, but to get medical backing for their own views. Whatever the doctor says they will report that he confirmed their opinion. If Mr Jones says, 'It's that terrible smell in the factory that's given me this chronic stomach' and the doctor says 'I'm sorry to hear that', he will be reported as saying 'The doctor said the fumes had poisoned my whole system'. Or if Mrs Jones says, 'Tommy got St Vitus dance because they caned him at school' and the doctor says, 'Hmmn', she

* Bourne, W. A. (1950) *Lancet* i, 127.

then reports this to her friends as 'The doctor said he'd never seen such a terrible case, and his nerves'll never be the same after that caning'.

In similar fashion those who wish to attribute illnesses to tonsils, air-raids, too much work at school, damp walls, or being dropped as a baby will seek medical support for their opinion. Many of these people deserve our sympathy and understanding. Surely it is infinitely more satisfying for them to rage at a bomb or to impugn a tonsil than to try to accept that some illnesses have no certain cause. Fate is such an insubstantial target for blame compared with a damp wall, a large tonsil, or a bad smell.

When a patient is seeking confirmation for an erroneous belief which does no one any harm and gives him the comfort of something to blame, it is questionable if much good is done in correcting him; but when he is out for blood, seeking ammunition with which to assail his employers, his doctor, or his hospital, then it is a very different matter. This is an age of compensation; not only out of loyalty to our colleagues should we decline invitations from patients to criticise each other, but for the good of the patients themselves. The psychological harm done to patients by long-continued litigation is even more extensive than the expense and trouble caused to the medical profession.

TALKING TO THE PATIENT

Having described some of the reasons why patients come to talk to doctors, I now consider some of the ways a doctor can talk to his patients. As I have remarked, this is not a subject that can be taught, but it can be discussed, and I will consider it under various headings.

First, *impressiveness.* The impression a doctor makes on his patient is as important as the pharmacological action of the treatment he gives, but a doctor wishing to impress a patient must consider first whether he is benefiting him. It is a good thing to give the patient confidence, but a doctor can pay more attention to the impression he is making on the patient than to the good he is doing him. Not only the way a doctor speaks, but his gestures, his manner and his smile all play their part. There are also accessory aids—a book written by the doctor himself lying carelessly on the desk, the use of a large shiny motor-car and chauffeur, or (less expensive but quite effective) the skilful manipulation of a really thick pair of horn-rimmed glasses.

Before using these adjuncts the doctor must consider whether he is trying to comfort himself or the patient. It is a greater medical triumph to leave the patient feeling better, but thinking little of the doctor, than to leave him worse, but deeply impressed.

Secondly, *tolerance*. For a successful doctor-patient relationship the doctor should try to achieve a level of tolerance and placidity nearing that of a saint. He must be free of prejudice and not let the patient or his relatives irritate him. Most of us have some foible, some little thing that rubs us up the wrong way. I knew one children's doctor who could not bear mothers who overdid the word 'little' as in the sentence: 'He draws up his little legs, doctor, and his little face is all screwed up when he passes his little motion.' I admit myself to an instinctive antipathy to patients who arrive for consultation chewing toffee or gum and also to patients who call me 'Doc'. Such prejudices can and should be avoided. The doctor's approach should not be 'Do I like this patient?' but 'Can I help this patient?' Experience will teach that many irritating mannerisms are caused by shyness and not by any desire to provoke; for instance the patient who remains apparently buried in his newspaper when the doctor arrives at the end of his bed is rarely reading it, he is probably assuming nonchalance because he is nervous.

Thirdly, *lucidity*. Misinterpretation of what the doctor says is so easy for the patient. Many a doctor who has given an explanation on which he prides himself would be disconcerted to learn the retailed version of his carefully chosen words. One lady told me she had taken her boy to hospital where the doctor looked down his throat and told her the ear-drum had grown right into the throat and was hanging out like a sausage. He cut it off and said if he'd been five minutes later the child would have been dead. I often wonder what he really said: I feel it cannot have been very clearly put.

Another example. Last week a woman attending my hospital for her gastric ulcer assured me the house-physician had provided her with a new medicine which consisted of a strong solution of rubber dissolved in orangeade which was designed to fill up the cracks in the ulcer and set. This purpose she told me had been achieved.

Both these patients were deluded but delighted; but harmful misinterpretation of doctors' remarks is even commoner. That is why lucidity is so essential. It is a difficult art to cut one's explanatory coat according to the intellectual cloth provided by the patient, and it must be especially hard for psychiatrists to word their interpretations without ambiguity, because the mind is even harder to explain than the body.

Fourthly, *confidence*. Confidence is an infectious thing—the doctor who possesses it is the doctor who can give it to others. It must be sincere. It is not much use pretending you are sure when you are not—the patient can tell. Confidence is invaluable because if you are certain you are right and if you can convince the patient that you are right then whether you really are right or not often makes very little difference. Yet the doctor should not assume omniscience. I have a notion that doctors do not often enough say 'I do not know'. It is better to tell a man confidently that you don't know than to tell him unconvincingly that you do. Patients can appreciate sincerity and truthfulness more than some people realise.

Another quality that helps a doctor deal with people well is *unhurriedness*. To give a patient the impression you could spare him an hour and yet to make him satisfied with five minutes is an invaluable gift, and of much more use than spending half an hour with him during every minute of which he is made to feel he is encroaching on your time. I do not know if this special kind of unhurried placidity can be acquired purposely, but it is a most enviable faculty to possess.

WHEN TO SPEAK

I now pass from the question of how to speak to the question of when to speak—in this case I mean when to probe beyond the purely physical side of a patient's illness. Physicians see a large number of patients whose symptoms are purely physically caused and respond completely to physical treatment. These require nothing except a prescription and a word of explanation. Then there are patients whose symptoms, although organically caused, seem to be giving them more distress than is warranted by their severity. Here it is well worth finding out what the patients' private beliefs about their symptoms are. Fear of a more severe disease than the one affecting them is in my experience a common reason for so-called functional symptoms. Many a young woman may complain of mild aches and pains which by themselves hardly worry her enough to be noticed, but because she has known somebody crippled with rheumatoid arthritis these symptoms cause her profound anxiety which itself provokes the symptoms further. Such women rarely mention their fear until it is sought out, but it is well worth seeking. There is often a sigh of relief and magical disappearance of symptoms when the patient is reassured that her fears are groundless. It is also just as common to find a man with unaccountable anxiety from minor symptoms because he has a fear of cancer. Here again the dread of cancer is elicited only by tactful inquiries. I think it is wise to ask all patients if they have any ideas about the cause of their symptoms and also to find out if they have any friend or relative suffering from a disease which they themselves fear. Strangely enough, those who have a dread of a disease seem rarely to be the people who suffer from it; so the proportion of cures by reassurance in this group is high.

Another type of patient where some probing may be rewarding is the hypochondriac—the patient who makes a hobby of doctors and drugs. The woman who keeps a diary not of social functions but of pelvic functions, the woman who instead of taking up canasta takes up her bowels and who patronises the great colonic laundries of Harley Street. If the doctor by his talk and his tact can interest her in the world outside instead of the intestines inside he will have achieved something really worthwhile.

CONCLUSION

The truth about doctor-patient relationships is, I believe, almost impossible to ascertain. We doctors rarely know what our patients think of us and rarely learn what effect our talk, tact, and treatment have had. 'He was so enthusiastic I didn't like to offend him' is commonly the attitude of the patient.

Occasionally, we get glimpses of the truth when we overhear a conversation on top of a bus or when patients' remarks are relayed to us by a friend (or more likely an enemy); but in the main we remain ignorant, and perhaps it is happier that we do so.

10

*The Dangers of Going to Bed**

It is always assumed that the first thing in any illness is to put the patient to bed. Hospital accommodation is always numbered in beds. Illness is measured by the length of time in bed. Doctors are assessed by their bedside manner. Bed is not ordered like a pill or a purge, but is assumed as the basis for all treatment. Yet we should think twice before ordering our patients to bed and realise that beneath the comfort of the blanket there lurks a host of formidable dangers. In *Hymns Ancient and Modern*, No. 23, Verse 3, we find:

> 'Teach me to live that I may dread
> The grave as little as my bed.'

It is my intention to justify placing beds and graves in the same category and to increase the amount of dread with which beds are usually regarded. I shall describe some of the major hazards of the bed. There is hardly any part of the body which is immune from its dangers.

Respiratory System. The maintenance of one position allows the collection of bronchial secretions, which, stagnating in the bases, encourage the development of hypostatic pneumonia. Further, the absence of exercise and the diminished respiratory excursion consequent on bed rest prevent the re-expansion of collapsed or diseased lung.

Blood Vessels. Thrombosis and thrombo-embolism are some of the most disabling and lethal catastrophes that bed rest can bring to a patient. The absence of leg movements means that the venous blood lacks the helpful squeeze from the muscles which normally speeds its flow, and the flexion of the thighs (particularly when there is Fowler's position or a knee pillow) obstructs it the more. One theory of

* Written for and published by the *British Medical Journal*, 13th December 1947.

phlebothrombosis is that it starts with endothelial damage caused by the weight of the leg on the bed compressing emptied calf veins. Thus, it may well be said that thrombophlebitis is the internal counterpart of the bed-sore. We may one day regard a thrombosis to be as much a sign of nursing mismanagement as we do the ordinary bed-sore to-day. It is significant that Hunter, Sneedon, and others, performing post-mortem examinations of the veins of the calf in middle-aged and elderly people who had been in bed a considerable time, found thrombosis of the calf veins in 53 per cent of the cases.

Skin. The frequency and dangers of bed-sores are too well known to need much comment. A large bed-sore in a heavy patient, especially an incontinent one, is a nightmare to the nursing staff, and the pressure points on the heels are often a source of great pain and misery to the patient even if the skin is still unbroken.

Muscles and Joints. The contraction of some muscles and the stretching of others are complications of rest which may cause considerable crippling. Foot-drop is, of course, the commonest, and stiffness and flexion of the knee-joints probably the next. The weakness and wasting of the general skeletal musculature and the restriction of the excursion of the joints are often manifest in the hobbling, painful gait of the convalescent patient.

Bones. When bones are not used the calcium drains from them, and this disuse osteoporosis can be a serious matter, especially in the elderly. Fractures for that reason may take longer to heal, and the absence of weight-bearing is another reason for delayed union. This is shown by George Perkins's recently published cases where the broken ends of bone, when splinted by a metal plate, did not heal until the plate accidentally broke and the resulting increase in weight-bearing led to rapid bony union. The advantages of the Smith-Petersen pin over older methods of managing intracapsular fractures of the femur are largely due to the shorter time in bed.

Renal Tract. The drain of calcium from the bones that I have just mentioned causes an increased liability to urinary calculi, and both kidney and bladder stones are sometimes in part due to bed rest. Far commoner than this is retention of urine. A patient, particularly a male, with a perfectly normal urinary tract can find difficulty in using a bottle—probably because of the horizontal position of the body coupled with the nervousness and embarrassment felt on attempting this unnatural, uncomfortable, and unfamiliar method of micturition. In older people this difficulty may lead to acute retention with overflow or to simple incontinence. Bed-sores may develop and keep the patient in bed, so initiating a vicious circle of bedridden incontinence. Prolonged incontinence leads to a deterioration of hygienic morale, and a patient may continue to be incontinent from sanitary sloth rather than urological disease. Getting a patient out of bed may turn him from an incontinent person to a clean one.

Alimentary Tract. This, too, is not immune from the bad effects of rest in bed. After a few days, minor dyspepsias and heartburn may be noticed; the appetite is often lost. Constipation occurs almost invariably, and even if not of grave significance is often a grievous worry to the patient. Its causes are, first, the absence of muscular movement; secondly, the change of environment (no one can say why this causes constipation, but it does); and, thirdly and most important, the difficulties of evacuating the bowel in a hospital bed-pan. On a bed-pan the patient is unable to use his abdominal muscles and his nearness to fellow-patients discomforts him. Precariously engaged in balancing himself, he sits there, poised unhappily above his own excrement in great dissatisfaction and distress. The constipation of bed rest is most harmful in the aged, where retained scybala may lead to a diarrhoea which marks the underlying obstruction. Retention with overflow is nearly as common at the back as in front. Quite often complete intestinal obstruction can develop from retained faeces, and when enemata fail to shift the scybala, digital removal has to be practised—a procedure as unpleasant for the evacuator as for the evacuee.

Nervous System. It is well known that, particularly in the ataxic diseases such as disseminated sclerosis or tabes dorsalis, even a short spell in bed may produce a deterioration of mobility which takes weeks to overcome, and any length of time in bed may leave a patient bedridden many years before the natural course of the disease would have made him so.

Mental Changes. Lastly, consider the mental changes, the demoralising effects of staying in bed. At the start it may produce fussiness, pettiness, and irritability. The patient may acquire an exaggerated idea of the seriousness of his illness and think, 'Surely I must be very ill if I am kept in bed?' At a later stage a dismal lethargy overcomes the victim. He loses the desire to get up and even resents any efforts to extract him from his supine stupor. The end results can be a comatose, vegetable existence in which, like a useless but carefully tended plant, the patient lies permanently in tranquil torpidity.

Even the insomnia and nocturnal restlessness so common in hospital patients may be related to the abuse of rest. Too much sleep during the day means too little sleep at night. You may notice that many patients who disturb the ward at night are flat on their backs snoring during the day. They lie in bed with nothing much to do, and we cannot blame them for taking frequent cat naps. I am sure that many hours of half-sleeping and dozing are less beneficial than a few hours of deep sleep, and I believe they encourage a certain confusion of mind.

So much for the commoner hazards of the bed. There are many I have omitted. I have not mentioned the loss of education in children who are long in bed, nor spoken of the dangerous dust that arises during bed-making, but even those evils I have outlined may help to show that rest in bed is anatomically, physiologically, and psychologically unsound. Look at a patient lying long in bed. What a pathetic picture he makes! The blood clotting in his veins, the lime draining from his bones, the scybala stacking up in his colon, the flesh rotting from his seat, the urine leaking from his distended bladder, and the spirit evaporating from his soul.

I have painted a gloomy and unfair picture: it is not as bad as all that. There is much comfort and healing in the bed, and rest is essential in the management of many illnesses. My object has been to disclose the evils of *over*dose, and I want now to indicate briefly how some of them may be avoided or overcome.

First, bed rest should be prescribed and not assumed—that is to say, a sister should not confine the patient to bed without the doctor's ordering it. Secondly, doctors should revise their attitude to rest where it is unsound. In a chronic ward of which I once had charge I found a lady who had been in bed for 17 years with a diagnosis of nervous debility and whitlow. She had survived this remarkable hibernation with little damage, and though she was very upset when I ordered her up she became a different person when she was fully ambulant. It may well be, too, that our attitude to rest in more acute cases could be modified. Rheumatic-fever cases are often kept flat on their backs for a considerable time, although there is no evidence that this modifies the incidence of heart complications and there *is* good evidence that the work of the heart is increased by the supine position. Patients with coronary thrombosis traditionally have six weeks in bed, but the evidence that this diminishes the incidence of complications is slender. Indeed, Sir James Mackenzie, who had frequent angina after cardiac infarction in 1908, never spent more than a few days in bed, but continued playing golf till his exercise tolerance at last became too small. He lived an active and useful life for 17 years after his first attack.

John Powers, of Cooperstown, New York, reported on 100 consecutive patients who were allowed to sit in a chair and walk on the first day after major operations. He compared them with an equal number who remained in bed for 10 to 15 days and found fewer complications in the first group. Further, the early ambulant cases were back at work within 4·8 weeks as compared with 8·7 weeks in the control group. All these facts encourage us to review the traditional amounts of bed rest that we order our patients.

The third way of avoiding the dangers of bed lies in altering the equipment and arrangement of a ward. There should be a day-room attached to every ward, and lockers for patients to keep their ordinary clothes in. Too often a sister puts all her patients back to bed as a housewife puts all her plates back in the plate-rack—to make a generally tidy appearance. Too often patients stay in bed because, shuffling round in slippers and dressing-gown, they are cold and uncomfortable. They would welcome a warm day-room with chairs and books. Some heart cases ought to be allowed to spend most of the day in arm-chairs and to sleep the night in them if they feel much more comfortable that way. For those that have to be in bed a commode might be allowed as an alternative to a bed-pan in most cases. More liberal attention should be paid to breathing exercises, limb-moving, and occupational therapy both to prevent complications and to distract the patient from going to sleep out of sheer boredom.

'Teach us to live that we may dread
Unnecessary time in bed.
Get people up and we may save
Our patients from an early grave.'

II

*Medical Salesmanship**

(*Nicolas Bentley drew the pictures*)

Doctors and members of a few other select professions depend entirely upon unofficial advertising. This demands a far greater subtlety of technique than does the commercial advertising in which other professions may indulge.

The man in the street believes that we made this decision as a modest piece of self denial, losing thousands of guineas in exchange for a little extra dignity. He knows little of the subtle ramifications of medical salesmanship and, luckily, he does not understand that our self-imposed ban on advertising is one of our most powerful advertisements; it suggests that we are a profession apart, a noble body of men who look on advertising as 'Such boastings as the gentiles use, or lesser breeds without the law'.

It is only in a journal circulating largely among medical people (I hope) that I dare assert that from the day we register as students our success depends on various forms of unofficial advertising; we constantly rely on salesmanship—putting across an idea, trying to convince, trying to get notice, blowing our own artfully muted trumpets with such subtle diminuendo that we hardly realise it. For a medical audience, salesmanship has to be restrained; Liberace when he enters a concert hall is illuminated by a battery of searchlights and at the same time several hundred doves are released into the auditorium. If one of the consultants arranged for a similar procedure to greet his arrival in the front hall there is no doubt it would make a deep impression, but critical remarks from other members of the staff would certainly be heard afterwards.

Medical salesmanship has to be most carefully adjusted according to the status of the salesman (student to consultant) and the stature

* Published in the *Middlesex Hospital Medical Journal*, Vol. 60, No. 1, February 1960.

of his clients: colleagues, patients, relatives or lay members of a committee.

THE STUDENT SALESMAN

The principal customers for the student's salesmanship are his teachers and his fellow students, but he also needs salesmanship in exams. He may be tempted by the enormous opportunities offered for impressing patients, but the wise student should avoid these,

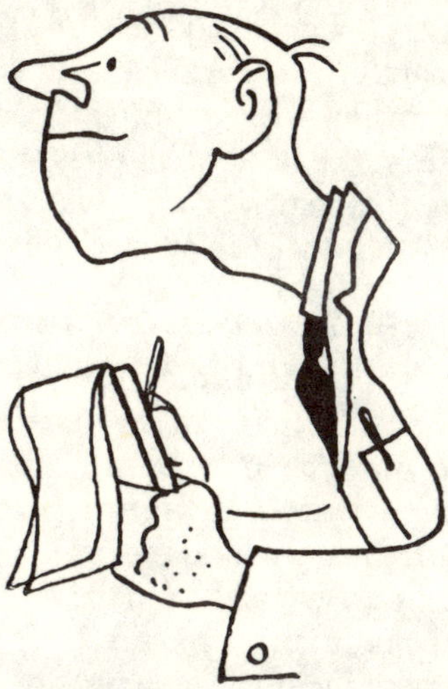

Do not thrust forward like an eager journalist

because when the chief next goes round the ward a few sarcastic words may destroy the impressive reputation he has built. He should not direct his salesmanship at patients, except occasionally just for practice. He must be content with studying the technique of his seniors; his own opportunity will come later. The main idea of students' salesmanship is to be noticed by the chiefs. The student who hopes to succeed has to become what Damon Runyon calls 'a guy who's around'—he has to be noticed and remembered. It is difficult because he must not be so noticeable that he seems ostentatious, nor so modest and unassuming that nobody knows who he is. He must manage by asking the right sort of questions on rounds and showing the right sort of prominence on the playing field or in the Christmas Shows. Questions are difficult; it is a great mistake to ask the chief something he doesn't know, but worse to ask him something he *does* know, but which he told you five minutes ago. It is best to ask about something he does know and that it is rather clever of him to know. To show that you are listening, an expression of respectful devotion may be helpful, but do not thrust yourself forward like an eager journalist, pencil and pad in hand, writing down every golden word that drops from the great man's lips. He knows some of his words are far from golden; he feels haunted and fears the words may be used in evidence against him later. 'Please, sir, that's not what Dr Carbuncle says. He told us that . . .', and the notebook is triumphantly produced. Head-nodding is a most unsatisfactory way of showing your attention; the monotonous to and fro motion coming from the head of an earnest student is irritating beyond measure; it may even drive a chief to avoid factual statements because he dreads starting the rocking mechanism.

SALESMANSHIP IN THE EXAMINATION ROOM

In order to pass examinations in medical subjects some knowledge is, unfortunately, necessary. But only quite a little. It is not the goods you possess but the way you put them in the shop window that matters. When doing a written examination remember that most examiners are in a hurry; they look at the beginning and at the end of the answer and do not scan every word in the middle of it. Therefore, if you are going to commit any atrocities bury them in the parenchym rather than expose them in the periphery. Do not put in pure padding; length without breadth is so easily seen. Even a tired or careless examiner will spot the excessive padding that makes an answer reek of upholstery. In *viva voce* exams it is always worth speaking as if you thought your answer was right, however uncertain you may be. If your answer *is* right, it spoils the effect to pronounce it with timorous vacillation. If it is wrong, it does no more harm to say it confidently and, if you say it confidently enough, you may convince a weak examiner that it is right.

It is important to remember that examiners themselves are salesmen, too, displaying their wares to their co-examiner and to the examinee. Do not try to get Sir Bernard Bronchus on his special subject, he may suspect you of toadying to him, for everyone knows he has been writing the same article about gall-stones for years; but if he happens to know about the different kinds of tapeworm or the causes of haematoporphyrinuria he will be anxious to display this surprising erudition both to you and to his fellow examiner.

The time waiting to enter the examination hall is good for practicing salesmanship on fellow students. It is useless poring over textbooks in the faint hope of reading the right bit, whereas an enormous impression can be made on fellow sufferers by doing a crossword or filling in a football pool entry while they are nervously riffling through the pages of their textbooks.

THE HOUSEMAN MUST WAIT

The Houseman has to keep most of his salesmanship for later use. His main duty is to provide a successful 'feed' for the salesmanship of his chief; yet he needs his own salesmanship when applying for

Give a dutiful laugh at the right moment

jobs, and, occasionally, when dealing with patients. A fellow houseman, with me at the London Hospital, was clumsy with his hands but quick with his mind; he had a clever phrase for use after failing to put a needle into a patient's vein. 'Now we do the other side', he used to remark in a satisfied voice; and the patient, if of moderately low mental calibre, would happily submit to what she believed was the other half of some bilateral investigation.

As regards the role of feed, this is one of the most painful duties a houseman has to perform. He must prove suitable entries for one of the half-dozen humorous stories in his chief's repertoire and give a dutiful laugh at the right moment so as to lead in the congregation.

Tedious as the role may be, it is worse for the registrar and worse still for the ward sister, both of whom have heard the stories many more times than the houseman. Have you noticed how registrars go to imaginary telephone calls, and sisters unaccountably go and take somebody's temperature at certain moments during the chief's round? Perhaps you can understand it now.

LOOKING FOR JOBS

Salesmanship in getting medical posts is a subject on which I have written already (*The Lancet*, 1st January 1949: 'How to apply for Medical Posts'). I wrote this anonymously because I did not want to

Some candidates gaze round them with a wild surmise

suggest that I had enormous experience of this subject. For the next few years I regretted writing the article, because most of the applicants for my registrarship or house job sent such alluring applications that to compile the short list was much harder. The most undistinguished career can be displayed in quite an attractive light if you know how to do it. The Hackenshaw Bradbury Prize for Biology, which you were grudgingly given at school (although there were no other entrants) because Colonel Hackenshaw Bradbury's widow wanted to present the prize herself, will look splendid in your application.

At interviews, the salesman applicant has to steer a course between spinelessness and cockiness. It is hard to look a Board in the eye, indeed it may have twenty eyes, and this makes some candidates, like Stout Cortez, gaze around them with a wild surmise, silent upon a seat in the Board Room (instead of a peak in Darien). Understatement of some major attribute is an excellent technique, especially if you have an ally on the Board who will drag the truth from you while you appear at pains to conceal it. For instance—

'Do you play any games, Dr Hercules?'
'Well, I play a little lawn-tennis, Sir.'
'Surely you were in the semi-finals at Wimbledon last year?'
'Well, yes, sir. As a matter of fact, I was. Absolute luck, of course. Can't think how I got there.'

'Nice young fellah that', mutters Lord Leptocyte under his breath, as you blush furiously and go out with the job in your pocket.

So you must hide your light under a bushel, but take care to see that your bushel is reasonably transparent.

THE EXAMINER SALESMAN

There is one hazard at interviews that it is impossible to surmount. That is internecine salesmanship—one member of the Board trying to impress the others. For instance, supposing during your interview you mention that you went to America.

'Did you see much of old Bolingbroke when you were at the John Hopkins?' he booms; 'I saw a lot of the old devil when I was lecturing out there last year . . .' and he reminisces interminably, not interested in you, but in displaying his extensive lecture tour and his intimate acquaintance with eminent people. If you give him no opportunity to display himself, he will crack jokes with his neighbour in a loud voice, so the rest of the Committee cannot hear what you are saying. The spectacle of Committee members showing off to each other is one of the most irritating ordeals a young doctor has to face. He can do nothing but grind his teeth. He is equally helpless with the witness-box type of interrogation in which he is expected to reveal his abilities by a series of yes'es and nothing more.

'You are Dr XXZ?'
'Yes.'
'I believe you qualified in 1950?'
'Yes.'
'You have just finished a job at St Quinidines?'
'Yes', and so on.

After a while you can try saying 'Yes' an octave higher or lower than is normal, which will make the interview less tedious, but it will not display your attributes any more fully. Nor will it help to try 'Indeed that is so', 'That is correct', and so on. This kind of chairman will still confine himself to asking for your assent to the facts you have written in your application and here again you can only grind your teeth.

THE CONQUEST OF SPACE

In senior salesmanship it is very helpful to acquire a really substantial entry about yourself in Churchill's *Medical Directory*. This is done not by the number of your accomplishments but by the way you set them out. If you have several long Christian names, mind you put them all in. If you have any distinctions to your credit, choose the long ones. 'The Barraclough-Ffarrowmere Memorial Prize for Research into Multiple Hereditary Haemorrhagic Telangiectasia' gives you much more space than 'M.D. Gold Med.' Remember this when you write a paper: 'A study of the Arthritic, Renal and Systemic Lesions in Human Podagra' may give you three extra lines, whereas 'Gout' achieves no space conquest.

The same applies to appointments. Phys. St Bart. carries much honour, but your other post of Assistant Geriatric Officer to the Hospital for Delinquent Deaf and Dumb must not be left out if you value your inches.

Next, your name itself is very important. If you have aspirations to medical greatness you may be hampered by a name like Brown or Smith. Do not despair, there is always a way out. The best thing is to dig out the most peculiar of your Christian names and join it to your surname with a hyphen. Though you were ashamed of being called Stramonium when you were at school (your parents hoped that your uncle would leave more to you in his will if they fell in with his wishes), now you are suddenly grateful (even though he left you nothing but that bronze card tray with 'The Rape of the Sabine Women' embossed upon it). Once you become Dr Stramonium-Smith, Dr Belladonna-Brown or Dr Rhabdomyona-Robinson, you can settle down to a life of assured prosperity. It is best to cement this felicitous union with a hyphen, or people will have difficulty in looking you up when they want to send you private patients. No one will remember that the famous Dr Charlatan-Slob is really just plain Dr Slob.

HOW TO IMPRESS PATIENTS

Impressing patients is a branch of salesmanship that is part of our trade. After all, we have to give them confidence in us. The best salesmanship cheers as well as impresses the patient. It is poor salesmanship to impress the patient with your own greatness, but leave him despondent about himself. Here is Bernard Shaw's description of that supersalesman Sir Ralph Bloomfield Bonnington:

> 'He radiates an enormous self-satisfaction, cheering and healing by the mere incompatibility of disease with his presence. Even broken bones, it is said, have been known to unite at the sound of his voice. His bland, voluminous energy imposes veneration and credulity on all but the strongest minds.'

The patient needing strong reassurance requires a consultant of overwhelming self-confidence and omniscience to convince him. I attempt to provide this in out-patients by a mode of behaviour I call

His bland manner produces veneration

'therapeutic iatromegaly', but before indulging in this deliberate self-aggrandisement I am careful to tell the students that I do not think as highly of myself as all that, much as I should like to do so.

Salesmanship is required, not only for reassurance but for treatment, the results of which largely depend on the salesmanship with which it is administered. The late Lord Duveen, whose salesmanship with pictures made him a large fortune, possessed this particular gift. When he took his small daughter to the seaside for the first time he exhorted her to paddle. She put one toe in the sea, said it was too cold, and refused to try any more. Lord Duveen gathered some driftwood and lit a fire. He filled the child's bucket with sea water and heated it until it was nearly boiling. Then he emptied the steaming liquid into the vast cold sea.

'Go on, try again now', he urged her. She cautiously tried one pink toe. 'Oh, thank you. That's much better' said she, and paddled happily for the rest of the afternoon. Much of our pharmacological treatment depends upon similar salesmanship by ourselves.

In salesmanship with patients, everyone finds their own technique. In capable hands the skilful manipulation of a really thick pair of horn-rimmed spectacles can work wonders. Another very effective device in private work is to demonstrate how aristocratic your clientele is. While you are talking to a patient your secretary enters timidly.

'Lord Podagra is on the telephone again.'

'Oh, tell him to go to the Devil', and you resume your conversation with a patient who by now is goggling with admiration.

Some patients might find this method frightening and a more friendly version of the gambit is worth knowing.

Enter timid (carefully rehearsed) secretary, as before.

'Excuse me, sir, but his Excellency, the Node of Tawara is on the telephone.'

With a muttered word of excuse you seize your telephone and burst out with:

'Hello, Noddy old man. In trouble again? That's too bad.'

THE HOSPITAL SALESMAN

Hospital work requires a different approach because there are nurses and students to impress as well as patients. I shall say rather little about it here, because you see it going on every day at hospital. Moreover, as a hospital consultant myself, I do not like to give away too many tricks of the trade. Two reliable techniques are: (*a*) feigned ignorance, and (*b*) eccentric behaviour. The technique of pseudo-ignorance is suitable for elderly men and starts with asking numerous artless questions, rather like certain Judges do.

'What is this free hydrochloric acid they mention in the report?', or

'Let me see now. What are these new fangled anticoagulants everyone is talking about?' and so on.

Then, after carefully building up an impression of helpless

senility you suddenly produce a sparkling, up to date dissertation on the tanned red cell agglutination test for autoimmune thyroid antibodies, revealing a knowledge of the very latest published and even unpublished work. The manoeuvre involves very little strain. You need study only one contemporary discovery fairly thoroughly to make it shine wonderfully against the carefully constructed background of senility.

Striding towards his Rolls, still in theatre boots

Eccentricity is a quality highly esteemed by students. Eminent professors are traditionally vague, and it pleases everyone if a surgeon puts on one theatre cap after another, forgetting that he has one there already, or goes out of the main entrance, still wearing his white gumboots, purposefully striding towards his Rolls Royce while the head porter respectfully tries to stop him.

Peculiarities of manner or dress are equally useful; carnations or orchids in the buttonhole have become too widely used to be very effective, but collars of an ancient style or elastic-sided boots may give pleasure to everyone. After all, if a consultant is perfectly normal there is nothing for students to imitate in the Christmas Shows, but generally by the time a man has become a consultant he has become peculiar enough to need no extra device. These natural peculiarities he cannot help, and it irks him to see them portrayed in the Christmas Shows. Yet he is so anxious to appear as 'a good sport' that the poor fellow has to swallow his shame and join in the laughter against himself.

THE ROSTRUM AND THE WRITING DESK

The esteem with which a doctor is regarded by patients and colleagues is much influenced by his written articles and his public utterances. This article you are now reading will not help my career at all and may even damage it. Certainly it will not encourage you to send me patients; it makes you think what a cynical heartless fellow I am. All the same, the fact that you have read as far as this means I have held your attention—and that is one of the objects an author strives for. If you want to make your readers think how modest and delightful you are you have to write in quite a different style.

Now supposing you are writing for the admirable purpose of getting yourself patients. You must learn what song writers call 'plugging'. Take any common complaint for which there is little effective treatment (for instance psoriasis, backache, or headache) and write an article suggesting you have found the treatment: 'A Hundred Cases of Backache Treated by Removal of the Sacrum.' Follow this up with 'Sacrectomy' and so on. It will be difficult to get these printed by respectable journals, but that need not bother you because doctors who read the lower-grade medical journals are just the sort likely to be impressed by scatterbrained schemes. Do not rest after publication, but continue relentless plugging in both the lay and medical press. Write to the daily papers criticising the Minister of Health because he has failed to provide for the enormous demands for sacrectomy then, when the time is ripe, found the British Sacrectomy Society, with you as its first President; follow this up with numerous letters to various medical journals suggesting sacrectomy as a cure for enuresis, migraine, advanced cancer or epilepsy, but always placing below your name the distinguished parenthesis: 'President of the British Sacrectomy Society'. Only when you are very firmly established should you found a weekly medical journal, *The Saturday Sacrectomist*, for the expense of having it privately printed is very great.

Physicians should use a similar technique, but instead of sponsoring a new operation they must advocate a new, expensive and almost unobtainable treatment. There are only three rules. First, the drug must be given by injection. Secondly, it must have a mysterious numerical name like Z.29, and thirdly, it should come from some attractive and unusual source, for example seeds found in the tomb of Nebuchadnezzar, or what about an extract of dormouse blood as a cure for insomnia? Though I promise you all these measures will fill your consulting room and bring you untold riches, you may lose the good opinion of your colleagues if you employ them all. The man who wishes his writing and utterances to stand at all high in the estimation of reputable medical men has to take a great deal of trouble. Many doctors have very little idea of how to write a presentable article and still less how to present a case or read a paper at a Medical Meeting. One day, if you want a serious paper from me, I will try to produce an article for you on: 'How to Speak at Medical Meetings', and 'How to Write Articles for Medical Journals'.

PER ARDUA AD ASTRA

I finish with a few general remarks for those who are aiming really high. Nowadays there are no sales prospects in general Medicine or general Surgery. If you want to reach the top, you must find a good selling line early in your career and stick to it. The more rarefied the specialty the greater are your prospects of early consultant status, but having reached your objective you must regard it as only the first step in your ascent to the stars. Having established your forward position, dig yourself in and erect fortifications. Separate yourself from lesser breeds like physicians and surgeons; do not have 'beds' or 'a ward'. If you have only three or four beds you refer to them as 'my unit', and when you get most of the beds in a ward you should call it 'my department'. You must strengthen your position by developing complicated and esoteric methods of investigation and acquiring an army of workers to perform them.

THE STRUGGLE FOR EXISTENCE

To rise quickly in your profession you must learn to sell your ideas by acquiring the technique of 'pseudo-profundity' or high falution. Remember that the harder anything is to understand, the more readily will committees allocate money to it. Much sensible medicine is obvious, but the obvious does not impress. If only you will trouble to learn the art of putting obvious or trite things in a quasi-profound way then the world will be at your feet. There is a more or less standard technique for turning the obvious into the profound and this process, which I have termed 'high falution', depends largely on using certain key words and expressions as often as you can. Here are the most important ones—

> broadly based, dynamic, integrated in perspective, stressor influences, unit, social economic and environmental condition, psycho-social, psycho-biological, psychodynamic (psycho-anything will do, except psychosomatic which is just a little overdone).

Do not study diseases, but 'observe the natural history of the disease' (heaven knows what the natural history is; I suppose it

The harder it is to understand—the more committees allocate to it

means 'what happens if you leave the patient untreated'). Do not study patients, but 'study the whole man' or, better still, 'view the individual in perspective against his economic and psycho-social background', or 'consider his dynamic status within the group'.

Let me explain. Any reasonable doctor when managing a patient takes into account what his home is like, what sort of family he has, and whether he is rich or poor. If Mr Jones lives in one room with five children, two cats, and a drunken slatternly wife, a sensible doctor would not order him to rest at home with two-hourly feeds of steamed custard. Nobody would be the slightest bit impressed if anyone explained these obvious things in a plain way, but if you follow my instructions and 'consider the patient as a psycho-dynamic whole, viewed as a socio-economic unit integrated within the cultural framework of his environmental and psycho-biological relationships' then everybody will be deeply impressed. I do not know why that is so, but it is true. The use of those key words lends an impressive but nebulous air of humane profundity to your utterances and conveys that ordinary doctors are unsympathetic and remote beings with no interest in their patients' feelings. I am afraid you may not believe me unless I give you some more evidence. Here is a paragraph from last week's *Lancet* written by a man who has started a new type of hospital in this country[1]—

> 'The methods are more than an alternative form of hospital organisation. They are based on the principle that the genetic and physical and the dynamic and psychological factors of disease are not opposites, nor even complementary but parts of a whole. Treatment must therefore include the whole social environment of the patient and all his social relationships. He must be treated not only as a person but as part of a community.'

Most of that means nothing at all beyond 'we try to deal with our patients' troubles and so help them get on better with the world'. Every reasonable doctor has been trying to do that for years, but because that man has used his key words properly he is making an enormous impression. Already he is director of an Institute, he holds an important lectureship, and discussions about building more hospitals of this kind are going on at the moment. You, too, can succeed like this if only you will follow my advice carefully.

Take another example. At the moment there is a scheme to talk to some blind children to find out whether their thoughts and dreams about things are affected by their being unable to see them. You may not think that sounds impressive, but here is the project written up in the way I have advised.[2]

> '*Content of Work.* It is a common assumption that visual impressions play an integral part in the individual's early content with his environment, i.e. in his object relations and the introjections and identifications built on them, as well as in the mental processes of memory, dream and fantasy life. Much additional information about this topic can be gained where the role of imagery is isolated by its total absence from the personality.'

Truly, these words are copied from the account printed in the *Proceedings of the Royal Society of Medicine* and already six people in a clinic are engaged in the work, which at present is only in the preliminary stage.

So much for the technique of high falution, or should I call it psycho-falution? I will give one more example of it; the title of an article that was published recently—'The Meaning of Postulational Psycho-physical Parallelism'.

I hope all these examples show you what wonderful effects can be produced by the skilful use of the right words and reveal that 'words of learned length and thundering sound amaze the gazing rustics ranged around'. My charlady once said to me, of someone she heard on her television: 'Oh, he's a real scholar he is. He talks so clever you can't understand a single word he says.'

THE SUPER SPECIALIST

Now though I have told you almost all these secrets of salesmanship that will bring you success in the Struggle for Medical Existence, you still need a word of advice about specialisation. As the new specialties become overcrowded the only sure way to get to the top is to invent new specialties yourself. We already have paediatrics (children), ephebriatrics (youths), mesiatrics (for the middle aged) and geriatrics (for the aged), but the seven ages of man are not yet completely covered and, even when every individual year has been claimed by the appropriate specialists, you can become an intermediatrician and develop a department to facilitate the difficult transitional period from one year to another.

Or supposing you want an entirely new line. As we even have special workers to manage the diversions that patients require to beguile the tedium of hospital life, there is an opening for a young man of initiative and enterprise to become the first ichthyologist and concern himself entirely with the subject of providing and maintaining the illuminated tanks of tropical fish which are so popular in hospital wards nowadays. You could start with a small department; yourself as the ichthyologist, and one or two ichthyographers under you, to chart the movements of the fish and record the head movements of the patients watching them. There would be an ichthyodietitian to supervise the production of fish food with a foreman formicarian under him in control of ants' eggs. Later, as you progressed in your work, an electroichthyologist for the electric eels and a radioichthyologist for the luminous fish would be needed. It might be several years before you got a complete Ichthyodrome to yourself, providing courses in psycho-ichthyology, ichthyodynamics and other essential matters, but, if you stick to it and work hard, there is little doubt there will be a College of Ichthyology in a few years' time; and, who knows, you, my dear reader, may become the first Senior Sturgeon or the Assistant Fishician.

That's all. I have told you all I know about salesmanship. Now go out into the world and practice it. Good luck to you.

REFERENCES

1. Joshua Bievev on 'Day Hospitals for Psychiatry', D. Soc. Sc., Vienna and director, Inst. of Social Psychiatry, *Lancet*, 1959, 2, 901 (21 November, 1959).
2. Hampstead Child Therapy Clinic (Anna Freud) Research Scheme, *Proc. Roy. Soc. Med.*, 1958, 51, 940, Number 11.

12

*Is Your Prescription Really Necessary?**

Is your prescription really necessary? What a lot of different things this can mean! Necessary for what? Necessary to whom? It depends, of course, on what you mean by necessary.

Is your prescription really necessary to ensure the continuing prosperity of drug manufacturers and chemists? Here surely the answer is an unqualified yes. Is your prescription necessary to convince your patients they are getting value for the money they contribute to the Health Service? Is your prescription necessary to get the patient quickly out of your consulting room so that you are ready for the next? It may take longer to convince a man he does not need medicine than it does to write him a prescription. Is your prescription necessary because the patient has read an article about a new drug and, like the baby in the advertisement, won't be happy till he gets it? Is your prescription really necessary because you don't like to admit to yourself you can do nothing (for instance, for the severe shortness of breath in gross emphysema) and does it give you the comforting illusion of doing something?

All those questions are likely to give us an uneasy feeling. I think the one most worth while discussing is: are most of the drugs we prescribe necessary?—by which I mean are they likely to benefit our patients?—and, even if they are, how often do they get the chance to do so? What proportion of drugs reach the stomach and what the sink? Are the form and the quantity we prescribe necessary in the sense that there is no unnecessary cost or extravagance—that smaller quantities or cheaper drugs would not have been so good?

First, the question of pharmacological usefulness. I know that large numbers of patients are given bottles of medicines for their coughs and I believe that in 90 per cent of cases the effect would be

* Published in *Medical World*, June 1960.

the same if an inert but portentously flavoured fluid was dispensed. Most of them depend on the action of expectorants (which have no expectorant action unless pushed to almost emetic doses). I don't know how many tonics are prescribed nowadays: I think they are less in favour than they were. As a child, I thought their purpose was to increase my appetite by giving me such a horrible taste in the mouth that I had to eat something to take it away. Though I have pursued a good many years of medical study since then, I know of no more plausible explanation today. There used to be a virtue in the sheer unpleasantness of medicine—a little of what you don't fancy does you good was the belief thirty years ago—but today the most unpleasant tasting substances, including dangerous and potent drugs, can be so skilfully doctored that young children frequently die of a surfeit of palatable elixir. Anyway, I do not think the prescription of tonics can be pharmacologically justified. Large amounts of liniment are still, I believe, prescribed and I have great doubts whether what is rubbed in makes the slightest difference. Certainly I know of no scientific work that shows it does. The rubbing itself may be beneficial.

Yet cough medicines, tonics and liniments are not usually very expensive and patients get considerable satisfaction from possessing medicines whether they are used for display as a bedside decoration which convinces their relatives they are ill, whether they place them in a medicine chest so that they all have to be taken out whenever anyone wants a bandage or a thermometer, or whether they really swallow a little before pouring the rest down the sink and using the bottle for french polish or turpentine.

It would take years to change the custom of the bottle of medicine. It is a deeply rooted tradition: mince pies for Christmas, medicines for coughs, champagne for weddings, liniment for rheumatism and so on. Prescriptions are shorter than arguments, and faith works wonders, so the provision of cough medicines, tonics and liniments will have to continue. They are socially, traditionally and psychologically essential however little pharmacological justification they have. So if we have to prescribe remedies whose pharmacological action is irrelevant, at least we should see they are harmless, cheap and provided in small quantities.

Next I turn to vitamins. We have all prescribed them, we will all continue to prescribe them, yet I believe over 99 per cent of our prescriptions are useless. Vitamins benefit only those who have been taking a grossly deficient diet and even then a return to normal diet would restore health nearly as quickly. There are a few exceptions. Certain intestinal diseases causing malabsorption of vitamins require treatment with them and lupus vulgaris responds to heroic doses of vitamin D—but for the rest there is little to justify the two million pounds annually spent on them. We probably feel that they cannot do harm and might do good and we get encouraging pamphlets from vitamin manufacturers. Many of us give nicotinic acid to anyone with a sore tongue. Probably not one in a hundred of those so treated receives any benefit because not one in a hundred of them has pellagra. Nicotinic acid cures the sore tongue of pellagra but does not cure all sore tongues just as quinine will cure the rigors of malaria but does not stop all rigors. The other vitamins are used equally irrationally, and because rats fed on a vitamin E deficient diet have miscarriages, vast quantities of vitamin E are doled out to barren women all over the country with no benefit to them. It does not fulfil the hopes of the poem I learned as a student:

Now Vitamins A, B, C and D
All keep us fit and strong.
But what's the use?
We must reproduce
Or the race won't last for long.
So Vitamin E's the stuff for me,
And it is plain to see,
We'll blast the hopes
Of Marie Stopes
By taking it with our tea.

I turn from the vitamins to the advertised proprietary drugs that greet us every morning at breakfast staring at us from the pages of our medical journals. We all prescribe a good many of them. Are our prescriptions really necessary? Let us consider antibiotics, hypnotics and haematinics.

Though many lives are saved by antibiotics, there is much evidence that by giving them too readily for trivial infections we kill the more susceptible organisms and so leave ourselves with the army of resistant organisms which now defy a large proportion of the antibiotics we use. This evil result is more likely to occur if we give the latest expensive antibiotic such as tetracycline when sulphadimidine would have done.

Hypnotics. This group is particularly vulnerable to the question, is your prescription really necessary? Not only could patients often recover without them, but frequently they are harmful. Many suicides are attempted with barbiturates and even if depressed patients need sedatives, they should be supplied in very small quantities. Hypochondriacs may become addicted to barbiturates and find that unless their lives are blunted by regular doses of amytal or phenobarbitone, they are never content. Even though the initial effect of sedation in a highly anxious neurotic is most satisfactory, some of them finish up in a worse state than they were before. If hypnotics have to be prescribed, they could surely be used more sparingly—for acute exacerbations of tension and anxiety, yes, but not often for continuous long-term treatment.

Haematinics. To treat anaemia rationally one hardly ever needs more than ferrous sulphate or gluconate tablets for the microcytic anaemias and B_{12} injections for the macrocytic. Rarely, folic acid is needed for the anaemias of pregnancy or steatorrhoea but this is a dangerous substance because when mistakenly given to people with pernicious anaemia it encourages the spinal cord damage. Yet many blunderbuss haematinic preparations are given, a number containing iron, B_{12}, folic acid, copper, vitamins, thyroid and heaven knows what. To use these preparations is irrational, extravagant and oftentimes unnecessary now that B_{12}, its active constituent, can be made cheaply and reliably. Even iron injections are rarely necessary except for the few people who cannot take iron by mouth or fail to absorb it when they do. The most extravagantly irrational practice of all is to treat a patient for anaemia for years without ever making sure that she has got anaemia at all, or ascertaining what kind of anaemia it is supposed to be. Anaemia is judged by the colour of the blood not by the colour of the patient. A drop of blood on blotting paper tested against a colour chart is quite a good test if more elaborate investigations are not available.

A good reason for prescribing proprietary remedies is that their names are usually short and memorable, whereas official non-proprietary drugs have long and unmemorable names. It is much easier to write 'Benadryl' instead of diphenhydramine hydrochloridum. The Ministry of Health could save millions of pounds by producing a preparation of asprin called simply Asp and another preparation of calcium aspirin entitled Casp, especially if they were brilliantly coloured capsules in decorative bottles rivalling the proprietary remedies in allure. I also wish the Ministry would produce an official inert tablet for our use with patients who need a pill to please them. We often waste active substances when we only want to please. Tab. Dulcis Fanny Adamin Co. might be a suitable name for it and it should be provided in a variety of attractive colours and shapes. This would save doctors from flinging the latest free sample of expensive proprietary pills at a patient who wants something new—a practice which often causes the patient to return in a week asking for more.

In conclusion, it may be more truthful to say 'our prescription is rarely necessary' rather than 'our prescription is really necessary' and there are certain things that can be done to improve the position.

1. Reform the bottle-of-medicine mentality by the right kind of propaganda.

2. Some sort of Gallup poll to find out what proportion of the drugs we prescribe ever reach our patients' stomachs. This would have to be carefully planned because our patients feel guilty as they pour away medicines (He's such a nice doctor I don't like to offend him) and it would have to be explained that the poll was secret.

3. More planned MRC investigations, such as those which assayed the effects of antihistamine drugs on the common cold and those which compared cortisone with aspirin, so that doctors get more reliable information about the most effective drugs.

4. A more critical appraisal of proprietary advertisements by the doctors who read them. Clinical trials are more informative than the wooing words and persuasive pictures of the glossy proprietary advertisements. If we are told that a substance is diphenyl-tetrahydroxazine-heptanone-hydrochloride and acts on the diencephalohypophyseal centres we must remain unpersuaded by this cannonade of rhetoric and simply ask 'Does it make headaches better?' We must not be like the country folk of whom Oliver Goldsmith wrote:

> While words of learned length and thundering sound
> Amazed the gazing rustics ranged around.

We must ask ourselves the question repeatedly and earnestly: Is your prescription really necessary?

13

*Malingering**

I do not want my contribution to consist only of anecdotes about malingerers, so I shall not spend long recounting stories of ingenious patients who fooled the doctors or tales of clever doctors and how they caught the patient in the act.

The pride of a doctor who has caught a malingerer is akin to that of a fisherman who has landed an enormous fish; and his stories (like those of fishermen) may become somewhat exaggerated in the telling.

Nor will I spend long on the details of technique: where the pins were hidden, how the blood was obtained, how the food was disposed of and how the thermometer was manipulated. These are matters of prestidigitation and are more worthy of consideration by the Magic Circle than by the Medical Society of London.

I am not going to confine myself to pure malingering, but I shall also discuss the borderland of malingering which provides even more difficult and obscure cases for study.

True malingering is defined in the *Concise Oxford Dictionary* as the pretending production or protraction of illness in order to escape duty, especially in soldiers and sailors. I allow a wider meaning to the term. To start with, I do not exclude the Air Force, especially as I remember an aircraftsman treated by Squadron Leader Harry Gosset who was a genuine haemophiliac and required over twenty pints of blood to stop the bleeding from his appendicectomy wound. This poor fellow, believing he was dying and wishing to confess his sins, admitted that he had simulated his appendicitis to get home for Christmas. He said he would never have done this had he known there would be so much bleeding trouble.

* Published in the Medical Society of London's *Transactions*, Vol. LXXV, 1958–1959.

I define malingering as the imitation, production or encouragement of illness for a deliberate end. The patient is quite conscious of what he is doing and quite cognisant of why he is doing it. With that definition, pure malingering—the planned fraudulent faking of illness—is, in my experience, a very rare condition. Either that, or else I am a very gullible physician. I know I have been mistaken before now and it is possible that many malingerers have deceived me without being suspected. I shall show you the portrait of a case where I was grossly deceived. It was over a matter of malingering associated with hysterical ataxia, scissor gait, and aggressive outbursts.

One Sunday, when my daughter was two years old, I promised my wife that, if it was not taken as a precedent, I would myself get her up from her afternoon rest, dress her and take her for a walk. I performed these duties without difficulty or loss of dignity, until the walk started. Then there was trouble. The child kept falling to the left; she walked with a ridiculous scissor gait and she frequently fell to the ground. She cried and said she had a pain. She behaved abominably, and I spent a wretched afternoon in Park Square West attempting to coax her into good behaviour. I knew this was sheer devilment, a malignant aggressive demonstration against the father figure; I would not submit.

At last my wife returned and undressed her for her evening bath. There was a sudden cry:—'Do you realise you've put both her legs through the same hole in her knickers?' I can still remember, after those tortured limbs had been freed from the crippling garments, how that gay, naked figure raced unrestrictedly to the bathroom without a trace of malingering. That incident taught me to be cautious about diagnosing malingering or hysteria. These diagnoses must not be made for the sole reason that the clinical picture is not yet hung in the clinical picture gallery of the doctor in charge. It may be something he hasn't heard of. There are too many examples of apparent malingering turning out to be cases of organic disease, and jokes about the high mortality of malingering or hysteria are commonplace.

I could show you a picture of a lady who had a lesion on her face and other lesions on her fingers and elsewhere. For a long time they were thought to be self inflicted, but biopsy studies have left no doubt that she is suffering from Phagaedena Geometricum of Von Brocq, and the control of the lesions by cortisone has brought great relief to the patient and to her doctor.

A young National Serviceman, who complained for over a year of peculiar abdominal pains, was thought to be malingering, but in the end he was found to have Von Recklinghausen's neurofibromatosis of the intestine, and several members of his family were discovered to be afflicted by the same rare condition.

Nevertheless, genuine authenticated malingering does occur. True malingering is best classified by motives rather than by techniques—the principal prime movers being Fear, Desire and Escape.

Fear: fear of call-up, fear of overseas duty, fear of warfare.

Desire: desire for compensation, desire for a comfortable pension, desire for revenge against a surgeon for some (usually imagined) wrong. Desire for the comforts of hospital life. Desire to stay in the ward longer because one has fallen in love with the staff nurse.

Escape: escape from a prisoner-of-war camp by incurable disability, escape from prison by transfer to hospital, escape from an impending court case, escape from battle.

Malingering by prisoners of war has evolved a variety of ingenious techniques, even to the extent of passing borrowed albuminuric urine, secreted in a false bladder and passed in the presence of a suspicious German doctor, through a hand-carved and hand-painted penis of life-like verisimilitude. The technical term for such realistic art is *trompe l'oeil*, an expression usually applied to oil painting but presumably correct for sculpture and wood carving.

It is well known that opposing forces try to weaken the enemy's army by dropping pamphlets persuading them to malinger. A particular pamphlet dropped in large numbers early in 1945 on English troops in Italy is worthy of your attention. Neatly produced in book-match form (to make it easy to hide), it opens with Three Golden Rules for Malingering which I do not think could be beaten:

1. You must make the impression you hate to be ill.
2. Make up your mind for one disease and stick to it.
3. Don't tell the doctor too much.

This pamphlet catered for all tastes and resembles the 'Do it Yourself' guides so popular to-day.

There is only time to give details about one of those. Here is how to have tuberculosis—according to the instruction book:

'First you must smoke excessively to acquire a cough. Then tell the doctor that you have lost weight, you do not feel well and that you cough a great deal. Say that sometimes you cough up streaks of blood. Sometimes you wake drenched with sweat. Stick to these symptoms, do not invent any new ones.

'Mix a very little blood with your sputum; suck it from your gums or a prick on your finger, one or two drops are sufficient.' Then there follow certain supplementary techniques of which I propose to omit the details. They concern the correct use of the smegma bacillus to enrich the bacteriology of the sputum. They are not attractive. The instructions finish with these encouraging words: 'All the above directions are based on scientific observations in well-known University Hospitals.'

The pamphlet was printed in the *Lancet* who gave it rather a discouraging review as follows: The authors would be disappointed to see how lightly their elaborate propaganda is received by our soldiers. They say they know far better tricks than these!

At Cardiff last week an ex-prisoner-of-war, Dr Archie Cochrane, told me a technique (he called it 'fudging' X-rays) whereby he annually returned three healthy prisoners to England totally disabled with radiological tuberculosis.

Painting in barium requires delicate brushwork very different from painting in oils. The technique of Van Gogh is useless for painting tuberculosis cavities however suitable it may be for sunflowers.

The general run of malingerers are of poor intelligence, and naïvety rather than ingenuity is the rule. Among ingenious and distinguished malingerers Sherlock Holmes is worth recalling. In 'The Case of the Dying Detective' Holmes had to convince Watson that he was dying of an obscure tropical disease. He started by reducing Watson's limited faculties to their lowest ebb:

'Facts are facts, Watson. You are only a general practitioner with very limited experience and mediocre qualifications. It is painful for me to have to say these things but you give me no choice. Shall I demonstrate your own ignorance?

'What do you know, pray, of Tapanuli Fever? What do you know of the Black Formosa Corruption?'

Mr. President, I do not wish to discomfort you in front of this distinguished audience, but can you improve on Watson's answer: 'I have never heard of either'?

After this preliminary humiliation Holmes had little difficulty in convincing Watson, who in his turn convinced the villain—Culverton Smith—that he, Holmes, was dying. At the end of the case when

Culverton Smith was in handcuffs and Holmes had revived himself with claret and biscuits, he described his methods: Three days of fast does not improve one's beauty. Then, with Vaseline upon one's forehead, belladonna in one's eyes, rouge over the cheek-bones and crusts of beeswax round one's lips, a very satisfying effect can be produced. A little occasional talk about half-crowns, oysters, or any other extraneous subjects produces a pleasing effect of delirium.

Mention of the imitation of delirium reminds one that mental as well as physical disease can be simulated. Those with little experience of mental disease may learn with surprise that it is very hard to pretend to be mad. For instance, the peculiar distorted thinking of the schizophrenic is something a sane person cannot manage. An experiment was done in which twenty normal people were asked to feign insanity; they, and twenty genuinely psychotic patients, were interviewed by psychiatrists (who had no other means of telling which was which). The psychiatrists were able to pick out the malingerers in nearly ninety per cent of the cases. Yet the most remarkable feat of feigning insanity was carried out by Lieut. Jones and Lieut. Hill who were prisoners in Yozgad, Turkey, in 1917. They were carefully coached by a fellow-prisoner who was a doctor and they went through almost unendurable privations in their successful pretence of madness. Their book, *The Road to Endor*, is still a best seller and a classic.

I now pass to those cases of illness which, though self produced or prolonged, do not constitute malingering. They do not have so definite a purpose. As you see, I have grouped them together as The Borderland of Malingering.

TABLE I

The Advantages of Illness

1. Illness as a Purpose (True Malingering)

---

2. Illness as a Comfort (Hysteria)	The Borderland of Malingering
3. Illness as a Hobby (Hypochondriasis)	
4. Illness as a Profession (Psychopaths)	

Hysterics differ from malingerers because, although they may produce illness and enjoy it, they are unaware of what they are doing. They possess a capacity for self deception; they can wall off part of their mind so that it is impervious to self scrutiny. This process, dignified by psychiatrists with the term 'dissociation', is coloquially called 'kidding yourself'. Some cases of hysteria are very close to malingering. Others start as malingerers, and as they become better at kidding others, they finally succeed in kidding themselves, and become hysterics.

TABLE II

The Borderland of Malingering

A. *Illness as a comfort*
   (*a*) Hysteria.
   (*b*) The Proud Lonely Person (Lucy's disease).

B. *Illness as a hobby*
   (*a*) The Grand Tour Type (rich hypochondriac).
   (*b*) The Chronic Out-Patient (poor hypochondriac).
   (*c*) The Eccentric Hypochondriac (faddist).
   (*d*) The Chronic Convalescent (daren't recover).

C. *Illness as a profession*
   (*a*) Anorexia Nervosa.
   (*b*) The Chronic Artefactualists.
   (*c*) Munchausen's Syndrome.

I have seen very little proven hysteria and I diagnose the condition only with diffidence. A fair proportion of 'hysterics' turn out to have organic disease, as many of us know to our cost.

Notice that among illness as a comfort I have put the proud, lonely person. Allow me to explain this. This pathetic type of case usually occurs in later life when praise and companionship are hard to come by. To lonely people a medical consultation may represent an event of great importance. It supplies that need to be noticed that exists in all human beings. A child cries: 'Look at my sandcastle!' A lonely old person cries: 'Look at my stomach.' The child says: 'I got two goals this afternoon!' The lonely old person says: 'I got two giddy turns this afternoon.'

I have heard from more than one practitioner of elderly people who have a weekly or fortnightly consultation of this kind. A visit from the doctor allows them the illusion of seeking medical advice rather than companionship. A patient may be too proud to complain of loneliness, but there is no loss of pride in complaining of symptoms. Lonely people miss, not only companionship, but also the advice and criticism that go with it. Under the guise of seeking advice about health, a lonely lady may be seeking advice about family affairs. Ostensibly she is asking for advice about her bad heart, but *au fond* she seeks advice about her bad nephew. This mild and most benign form of malingering, in which solitary elderly people look for company or counsel under the thin disguise of chronic ill health, is understandably tolerated or even enjoyed by quite a lot of practitioners. It could well be called Lucy's disease after Wordsworth's Lucy:

> 'She dwelt among the untrodden ways
> Beside the springs of Dove,
> A maid whom there were none to praise
> And very few to love.'

Turning to the hypochondriacs, first we have the rich hypochondriac. I call this one The Grand Tour Type, because she spends much of her time touring the larger cities in Europe visiting consultants. She always carries a large dossier, opinions from consultants, X-rays and laboratory reports; and usually a list of her own symptoms which she has carefully written out. During her tour she may have persuaded surgeons to remove some of her less essential organs. She has usually had her gall bladder and a quota of her pelvic organs removed by the time she reaches one's consulting room. Such women discuss consultants with their friends as one recommends a fashionable tailor or a smart hairdresser, and rival each other in the grandeur of the consultants they have visited as well as in the complexities of their investigations and treatments. They are usually married to rich but unattentive husbands who supply them with money for their hobby as a substitute for affection. To the consultant in private practice they are a familiar, tedious and lucrative burden.

The poor hypochondriac (or perpetual out-patient). Every hospital has a number of out-patients who have attended for many years. Whenever they are discharged from one department they turn up in another, thus acquiring a very large collection of documents, rivalling that of the rich hypochondriac although written on less luxurious writing paper and penned by less illustrious names. Though some have genuine chronic illness, many of them attend because they like the companionship of hospital; instead of going to the local public house for a glass of beer and a chat with the landlord, they go to the local hospital for a bottle of medicine and a chat with the other patients. One enlightened doctor tried the experiment of arranging out-patient sessions where the patients did not see the doctor at all unless they asked for him. It was a great success.

The eccentric hypochondriacs. These people like peculiar or

unorthodox treatments. They like so-called 'natural' things and belong to the homespun, wholemeal, handicraft school of living. They know a clever little man who can find out what is wrong with you by holding a pendulum over you or using some form of magic box. They believe with apostolic fervour in nature cures, osteopaths, astrologers and herbalists. Their preoccupation is more with treatment than with illness and they are harmless and often entertaining.

The chronic convalescent. When a patient has had longstanding organic disease for many years it becomes so familiar to him that it is almost a friend. If the illness is suddenly cured, he may feel deserted and friendless. He misses the familiar pain, the sympathetic enquiries of his friends and the security of his medical routine. He feels like a man who has worn shoes so long that he can no longer go barefoot. He does not really want to get well; he has become a hypochondriac.

Now the last group: Illness as a profession. First, I consider anorexia nervosa. The reason why these people go to such lengths to avoid eating is rarely clear. They will resort to a variety of artifices to avoid food. They will hide food in their bed lockers, pour milk into their hot-water bottles and insist on starving in the midst of plenty. As a result of the starvation, amenorrhoea is an early symptom and this formerly led to the illness being confused with Simmonds disease, with which it has nothing to do.

The next group is that of the chronic artefactualists, who may spend years in self mutilation or the production of spurious fevers. Skin diseases are most favoured by the sufferers from chronic autogenous disease, but various other forms of self-damage are reported. A group of nineteen patients was reported by workers in the Psychological Medicine Department of the Birmingham Hospitals under the title 'Deliberate Disability'. Their most surprising finding was that most of these patients are highly intelligent. One possibility is that their intelligence prevents them from learning the art of hysterical dissociation. One young woman was referred to me by Dr Harold Wilson. She was a bit of a problem child; she had been more or less bald for several years and he suspected the condition was due to trichotilomania (dermatologess for hair-pulling). He suggested that hypnosis, which is a part-time activity of mine, might stop her. At our first interview I asked her if it was possible she was occasionally pulling hairs out of her scalp. She said, yes, she thought she was. I then said as it seemed to be making her bald it might be a good idea to stop pulling her hair out. She said, all right, she would try. That was the only treatment given. I never used hypnosis on her at all and yet she had a normal head of hair within three months.

Lastly, Munchausen's syndrome. This is the strangest and rarest form of chronic autogenous disease. I described and named the syndrome in a paper (*see* page 170) in the *Lancet* seven years ago, but it had been recognised for generations; all I did was to provide a convenient label.

TABLE III

Munchausen's Syndrome

Three main types

A. Laparotomophilia migrans.
  With mainly abdominal symptoms.

B. Haemorrhagica histrionica.
  Colloquially—'haemoptysis merchant,' 'haematemesis merchant.'
  Largely specialising in haemorrhage.

C. Neurologica diabolica.
  Specialising in faints, fits, stupor, etc.

The patient with this syndrome is nearly always brought into hospital by police or bystanders, having collapsed in the street or on a bus with an apparently acute illness, supported by a plausible and yet dramatic history. Though his history seems most convincing at first, later his story is found to be largely false, and his symptoms and signs mostly spurious. He is discovered to have attended and deceived an astounding number of other hospitals. At several of them he may have been operated upon, and a large number of abdominal scars is often found. So skilfully do these people imitate acute illness that the diagnosis may be quite unsuspected until a passing doctor, ward sister or hospital porter says 'I know that man—we had him in St Quinidines last September. He says he's an ex-fighter pilot shot in the chest, in the last War, and he coughs up blood; or sometimes he's been shot through the head in the last war and has fits.'

Common varieties are—

(*a*) The abdominal type: laparotomophilia migrans.

(*b*) The bleeding type: haemorrhagica histrionica, colloquially called haematemesis merchants, haemoptysis merchants, and so on.

(*c*) The type specialising in faints, fits, convulsions and paralysis (neurologica diabolica).

These people differ from other chronic artefactualists in their constant progression from one hospital to another, often under a variety of false names, but nearly always telling the same story. They rarely stay at one hospital for long, but, if not already ejected, discharge themselves within a few days and off they go on their wanderings, deceiving one hospital after another, telling the same false story, faking the same fictitious symptoms and submitting to innumerable operations and investigations.

Almost all of you have encountered examples of this, but I still say it is rare. It seems common because the afflicted (or afflicting) patients never stop working for a moment. One patient may visit over fifty hospitals in a year. With Munchausen's syndrome a little goes a long way, or, as Churchill might put it: Never in the history of medicine have so many been so much annoyed by so few.

The term Munchausen's syndrome is not beyond criticism and various other names, such as Hospital Hoboes, have been suggested, but the term is convenient and seems to stick.

The gentleman to whom I respectfully dedicated this syndrome originated as a real person—Hieronymus Karl Frederick Von Munchausen of Brunswick—who was wont to entertain his friends by recounting fabulous adventures of palpable absurdity. When Rudolph Raspe of Hanover anonymously published these stories without his permission, a gentlemanly old fellow with a gift for tall stories became the laughing stock of Europe and the eponymous representation of an incorrigible liar. It is to Raspe's fictitious Baron that my term refers; the patients resemble him in the dramatic nature of their stories, the wide extent of their travels and the untruthfulness of their tales.

I must tell you one of Baron Munchausen's stories, for they are truly splendid. The Baron tells how he was out hunting one day and, just when he had used up all his shot, he met a huge stag. In this emergency he charged his gun with cherry stones and let fly, hitting the animal in the forehead. The stag was momentarily stunned, staggered a few paces and made off into the forest. Two years later he was out hunting again when he encountered a particularly noble stag. Luckily on this occasion he was better equipped with ammunition and, after despatching the beast, he lunched off haunch of venison with cherry sauce, for there was a flourishing cherry tree growing from the beast's head.

The stories told by Munchausen patients are equally untrue, but less inherently unlikely; indeed it is the credibility of their stories that makes these patients such a perpetual and tedious problem.

It seems that nothing can be done to prevent their continuing clinical depredations. Most doctors are so pleased if they succeed with detection and ejection they never think about protection. Though serious psychiatric studies of these people have been made, nobody can yet answer the two fundamental questions:

(*a*) Why do they do it?
(*b*) How can we stop them doing it?

It is lucky there are so few of them.

All that can be said about them, and indeed about the whole subject of malingering, are these words of Robert Burns:

'But human bodies are such fools
For all their colleges and schools
That when no real ills do perplex them
They make enough themselves to vex them.'

Shall we leave it at that then? The best explanation for all this self-manufactured disease is simply this: That human beings are such fools.

14

*Diseases Caused by Doctors**

Although textbooks of medicine devote a section to each of the known causes of disease—bacteria, parasites, deficiencies, and so on, no textbook that I know of has yet devoted a section to this large and important group of illnesses. As doctors we probably do not like to admit to ourselves that we cause illnesses as well as cure them. Nevertheless, at a time when medical science proceeds faster than ever before, and advances and discoveries crowd upon each other, it behoves us, when reviewing the balance sheet of medical progress, not only to look at the credit side but to cast our eyes critically and honestly down the debit column.

It is sad that almost every major advance has either a mental or a physical illness indirectly attributable to it and every therapeutic weapon can harm as well as heal; for example, the invention of the stethoscope by Laennec was a great contribution to cardiology but contributed also to cardiac neurosis. Young people with healthy hearts have, because of an innocent systolic murmur, been cautioned and cosseted into a state of chronic invalidism. Hearts should be judged by what they can do and not only by the noises they make.

Riva-Rocci, when he made the first sphygmomanometer meant no harm to anyone, but if he could see the results of the excessive use of that instrument he might grieve indeed. The anxious business man who pens the latest figure in his diary each week and whose spirits rise or fall when a few millimetres are lost or gained may have been a carefree man before his blood pressure was taken. Assuredly, the chronic trepidation with which he awaits the weekly reading is the one certain way of increasing his blood pressure. A doctor can thus become guilty of treating a fluctuating column of mercury instead of a person.

* Published in *Medical Excerpts*, date unknown.

Preoccupation with the bowels is a common complaint and often initiated by the doctor. If a doctor asks about bowels before anything else the patient soon begins to feel that something dreadful will happen if his bowels aren't open every day. This idea, once founded by the doctor is fostered further by some of the advertisements in the daily press, and the patient begins to think of his inside as full of potential poisons and starts to insult his intestines with irritating purgatives in a futile effort to 'cleanse the system'. Should his abused alimentary canal try and snatch a day's rest from the unnatural activities forced upon it, this is at once regarded as dangerous constipation, more purgatives are taken, and the vicious circle started again.

Turning to the more physical illnesses produced by doctors the most striking example is serum jaundice. Here we have a disease which could not exist without doctors, because it is transmitted almost entirely by injections or transfusions. The first cases were often dismissed as arsenical jaundice when they occurred in V.D. clinics, and on other occasions were regarded as infective hepatitis. It is now known beyond doubt that serum jaundice is a separate disease; the virus is present in both serum and nasopharynx but not in the faeces and urine; and the incubation period is 25 to 35 days. Serum jaundice is not usually serious, but as death from hepatic failure can occur in the acute stage and cirrhosis of the liver can follow after the acute stage has passed, it has to be recognised as potentially dangerous.

Serum jaundice is not the only new disease which transfusions can produce. Erythroblastosis foetalis is a more important one. If a woman has no rhesus positive cells in her, when she is transfused with such cells her blood soon makes antibodies against them, and if she later carries a child who has rhesus positive cells her own blood reacts against that of the child within her; because of this the child may be stillborn, or else be born suffering from erythroblastic anaemia, severe jaundice or oedema. This heavy penalty for a possible life-saving transfusion need never be inflicted. Any woman who is a potential mother should have her blood tested for the rhesus factor before transfusion, and if she has no rhesus positive cells she should never be transfused with any blood that contains them. This fact is simple but is unfortunately smothered by many recent articles about the rhesus factor which concern themselves with its rarer subgroups and indulge in petty quarrels over their extremely complicated nomenclature. The experts may quibble about $R_1{}^wR_2$ and C^wDe/cDE

but the practical doctor must learn that the rhesus negative woman must never be given rhesus positive cells.

Lastly, we come to the biggest source of iatrogenic (doctor-induced) diseases—drugs. It is a wise physician who knows as much about the dangers of the drugs he uses as he does about their good effects. Knowledge of good and knowledge of evil ought to be learned together as Adam and Eve learned them. It is, of course, impossible to list all the toxic effects of drugs, but it is worth looking at some of their graver disadvantages.

Bromidism, particularly in elderly or hypertensive people is a serious disease easily mistaken for senile dementia. Many doctors expect there to be a bromide rash with it, whereas this is exceptional. Quite small doses of bromides given for several months accumulate steadily, replacing the sodium chloride in the body by sodium bromide. When the blood bromides rise above 200 mg/100 ml, mental symptoms almost always occur with confusion and hallucinations. This results in more bromides being given to quieten the patient. I have seen quite a number of ostensible senile dementias where bromides were regarded as the treatment of the illness, though in actual fact they were the cause of it.

Atropine is dangerous in old people to whom it is often given when they suffer from Parkinsonism. Though large doses may relieve the spasticity of the illness there are two major dangers. First, the dilated pupil means that the bunched up muscles of the iris obstruct the normal drainage of the eye—the internal pressure increases and glaucoma results. Secondly, and this is not generally recognised, large doses of atropine produce a state of delirium with excitement and disorientation and, as with bromides, this condition can wrongly be diagnosed as senile dementia. John Gerarde in his Herball of 1597 wrote of belladonna: 'It troubleth the mind, bringeth madnesse if a few of the berries be inwardly taken.'

Opiates if used excessively by the doctor may start a habit of drug addiction, but most physicians are probably more frightened of producing addiction than they need be. Drug addiction tempers the wind of reality to the psychically shorn lamb, and it is only with neurotic patients that doctors must be careful in giving opiates. All the same it is alleged that the evil caused by heroin is greater than the good it does and some suggest abolishing its manufacture altogether.

Many newly-discovered drugs have their dangers too. The new antithyroid drugs of the thiouracil group occasionally have a serious toxic effect on the white cells. Even frequent white cell counts do not exclude this danger, and tragic cases of fatal agranulocytosis still occur. Folic acid though a major advance in the treatment of sprue, has the peculiar property of treating the blood changes of pernicious anaemia without any effect on the spinal cord changes which are part of the disease. Its use in pernicious anaemia might thus be an effective way of producing subacute combined degeneration of the cord, because the satisfactory blood picture blinds the physician to the progressive degeneration in the nervous system.

As regards streptomycin in tuberculous meningitis, it is unfortunate that doses large enough to produce a cure are often toxic enough to harm the patient, and intractable vertigo and deafness are common and, on occasions, blindness and mental deterioration have been produced.

Listing these toxic effects one after the other gives an impression that there is a sort of tax on progress and that every treatment produces diseases as a by-product. That is quite untrue. Penicillin, for instance, is almost entirely free from toxic effects, and nowadays so much time is spent in laboratory tests to find out the potential dangers of new drugs that in future all drugs will probably be safer and safer.

A rather cynical but cheering thought is that the illnesses caused by drugs may indirectly benefit the patient. A patient with mild rheumatoid arthritis may develop extensive dermatitis and possibly agranulocytosis if he is given gold injections. He will then be given BAL intramuscularly to treat his gold reaction, and in consequence acquire a sterile abscess of the buttock. After many weeks in hospital he is so grateful to have recovered from his dermatitis and his abscess that he has almost forgotten about his rheumatism. There is partial truth in the statement 'if you can't cure the patient of his disease, give him another disease and cure that'.

15

*Straight and Crooked Thinking in Medicine**

As doctors we like to be men of action as well as thinking men, but, however much we act, every action is preceded by a certain amount of thought—or ought to be. It is worth paying attention to the way we are thinking, studying whether our reasoning is sound or unsound, whether we have any faults of thinking, whether we are unconsciously using methods of thinking which are illogical or even irrational, and seeing if we can improve the quality and effectiveness of our thought.

Thouless in his valuable book, *Straight and Crooked Thinking*, classifies thirty-four dishonest tricks of argument (and very ingenious they are too), but his work is largely devoted to political thought—a field in which the quantity and variety of crooked thinking are of quite a different order from those of medicine. In considering medical crooked thinking, I have purposely not used much systematic classification, because one form of crooked thinking common in medicine is caused by overclassification and the forcing of facts into the compartments provided for them, whether they fit or not. I am therefore considering straight and crooked thinking in medicine under the heading of therapeutics, statistics, causes, words, etc., but without formal classification.

Most medical thinking is based roughly on formal logic, a subject which is rarely studied to-day, though it is used unconsciously in much of our reasoning. Logic teaches a man to recognise what conclusion can be drawn from a series of statements (called premisses), and if logic is correctly applied to true statements it must infallibly follow that the conclusion drawn from them is correct. For instance,

* The Chairman's address to the Middlesex County Medical Society on 24 September 1953 and published in the *British Medical Journal* in August 1954.

if we consider the two premisses (1) all cats are mammals, and (2) all mammals have hair, then it follows inevitably that all cats have hair. Those of you who have learnt formal logic will recognise this as a syllogism in the mood of Barbara. Similarly, if we take the statements (1) all cats are quadrupeds, and (2) all dogs are quadrupeds, it does not follow that all cats are dogs, because there is what logicians call an undistributed middle term—the term quadruped is not distributed entirely to dogs—only some quadrupeds are dogs, not all of them. The use of logic can be extended to cover a much larger number of premisses. Here is an example with three premisses from a book of logic: (1) no one takes in *The Times* unless he is well educated; (2) no hedgehog can read; and (3) those who cannot read are not well educated. From this it follows conclusively that no hedgehog takes in *The Times*.*

THERAPEUTICS

In medicine, most of our premisses are the facts found by research workers, and many of the conclusions from these facts become translated ultimately into ideas about the cause and treatment of disease. Research proceeds now at so great a rate that it is essential that reasoning must keep pace with factfinding. As much trouble must be taken in reasoning from facts as it is in establishing their truth. Though medical data may not always be subjectable to the rigid application of formal logic, most views on therapy have behind them some attempt at a logical argument. The premisses and the arguments are not always expressed openly, so that crooked thinking is often concealed behind an impressive and persuasive array of words (particularly in brochures accompanying proprietary remedies). It is a profitable and useful exercise for all those who wish to think straight to analyse reasoning and weigh evidence by exposing the bare bones of an argument, and see how it looks. Do we not sometimes find that we are being influenced by arguments of this kind: (1) small people do not grow enough, (2) anterior pituitary makes rats grow, (3) therefore small people need anterior pituitary; or of this sort: (1) pregnant rats without vitamin E miscarry, (2) therefore women who miscarry need vitamin E?

Let us consider some of the premisses again. (1) Anterior pituitary

* This example is quoted from Lewis Carroll's *Symbolic Logic*, which is recommended as a diverting book providing stimulating exercise in logical thinking as well as a refreshing allowance of Carrollean humour.

makes rats grow. Can we deduce anything from this? Can we even say because anterior pituitary makes rats grow that undue smallness in rats is due to lack of pituitary. Not necessarily, although it sounds quite reasonable. We are really saying if A causes B, then lack of A causes lack of B. Let us try this argument on something else. By the same process of reasoning we can argue living at a great height causes polycythaemia, therefore anaemia is caused by living at a great depth. Can we even argue that, because rats deprived of vitamin E miscarry, giving vitamin E to rats will prevent them miscarrying? If lack of A causes B, will plenty of A prevent B? Again a little thought will show how fallacious this argument is—for instance, lack of water causes rats to die, but giving them plenty of water will not make them immortal.

I am not arguing from this that pituitary extracts have no place in the treatment of dwarfism, nor vitamin E in the prevention of abortion, but I do say that a very different set of premisses and deductions are needed to give a logical basis to their use.

The logical approach to therapeutics is first to make a hypothesis from available facts from which we can deduce that some substance might benefit a condition, and then proceed to a controlled clinical trial to find whether it really does do so.

In other words, when we consider a line of treatment we start with the question 'Should it work?' and finish with the question 'Does it work?' Too many treatments are still advocated merely because there is a theoretical reason why they should work and without a practical controlled test being done to see whether they do work. For instance, because creatine excretion is increased in muscular dystrophy and glycine by mouth increases the supply of creatine to the body, the administration of glycine to sufferers from muscular dystrophy was advocated for a good many years without any convincing evidence that it was effective.

Are we not prone to accept a drug as effective in treatment because it ought to work rather than because it does work? Undoubtedly we are. Is there not a tendency to be convinced that because a drug reduces gastric acidity it does heal gastric ulcers, that because a drug increases cardiac output it benefits cases of heart failure, or that because a drug kills micro-organisms in a Petri dish it will kill them just as well in a living patient? The theoretical and laboratory tests for the effects of treatment are an essential part of clinical research and are responsible for many brilliant advances in therapeutics, and doctors must be on guard against being converted too readily to a line of treatment by theoretical arguments until these are supported by practical clinical tests.

CLINICAL TRIALS

When we are organising practical clinical tests is it not crooked thinking to assess the success of treatment by measurements of associated factors not intimately related to the disability? Splenectomy, for instance, may be highly beneficial in cases of congenital haemolytic anaemia, yet measurement of the fragility of the cells after splenectomy would show no improvement. Phenylbutazone may relieve a man's rheumatism enormously without necessarily bringing down his sedimentation rate.

There is no illness in which clinical improvement has been so variously assessed as in rheumatoid arthritis. As well as sedimentation rates we have instruments to measure the angular range of movements, graduated metal rings to measure the circumference of joints, dynamometers to measure the strength of grip, eosinophil counts to see what cortisone is doing to the blood, and yet anyone who has worked for long with rheumatism finds all these tests of little value compared with the direct measurement of the disability. Here in the cortisone clinic we may record weekly the time a patient takes to button up her stays or to lace up her shoes. We see how long she takes to walk the length of the ward, and note whether she can brush her hair or peel her potatoes.

Perhaps to younger people these tests seem less scientific because of their homeliness, but there is really nothing unscientific about them. Helmholtz said that all science is measurement, and many of these homely data can be measured quite informatively—the volume of soup spilled by a patient with tremor can be measured, the time to do up buttons can be charted, the amount of potatoes peeled in a standard time can be weighed, and so on.

Another error of thinking which profoundly influences therapeutics is to believe that improvement after treatment is due to treatment, the *post hoc ergo propter hoc* argument. Stated as bluntly as that, it seems obviously invalid, but hundreds of remedies are advocated on little better argument. In truth, the reasons a man may feel better after a pill are numerous—he might have felt better anyway, he might have felt better because he had such faith in the pill, he might have felt better because you had such faith in the pill, or he might really be improved by the pharmacological action of the pill. The best evidence of the effectiveness of a remedy is to have randomly allocated groups of patients—one treated with the substance, one with its inert counterpart—and nobody (doctor, nurse, or patient) having any idea which is the treated and which the untreated group. Now, the nature of treatments and the numbers of patients with particular illnesses make such ideally controlled experiments not always possible, but there are many treatments in common use to-day which have never been subjected to such testing—many drugs whose efficacy has never been scientifically demonstrated.

Use of Vitamins

If I had to suggest one particular field of therapy which needs to come under the scrutiny of statistical clinical trial it is the use of vitamins. More than two million pounds' worth of vitamins are prescribed each year under the National Health Service, and evidence that they do much good is very scanty. Are we not accepting arguments of this kind: (1) people deprived of vitamin B have sore tongues, (2) therefore everyone with a sore tongue needs extra vitamin B; (1) people deprived of vitamin C heal their wounds slowly, (2) therefore everyone with a wound needs vitamin C. These arguments alone are not rational—for instance, people deprived of salt for long enough may become mentally confused, but not everyone who becomes mentally confused needs salt.

The laity, too, have got the idea that as vitamins are essential to life any food that is full of vitamins is extra good for them. Subconsciously, I think they have adopted a sort of mathematical crooked argument that A is good, therefore 2A is twice as good and infinity × A is infinitely good. This is a dangerous argument. Cobalt, for instance, is (in minute quantities) essential to life, so is sulphur, yet a diet saturated with these substances might prove fatal. An even more dangerous use of the argument that 2A must be twice as good as A is, if one person has a moderate supply of wisdom and administrative ability, that ten people (that is to say, a committee) will function with ten times that wisdom and administrative ability. Those of you who have tested this hypothesis in practice know how sadly untrue it is.

But to return to vitamins—the reason why they provide such a glorious field for the polytherapist and the commercial chemist is that they are more or less harmless (apart from very heavy doses of vitamin D). Therefore any doctor can prescribe them with the argument, 'If you have vitamin deficiency, they will do you good; if you haven't vitamin deficiency, they can't do you harm—therefore logically we might as well prescribe them for everyone'. This argument is dangerous for these reasons: (1) by extending the argument we would find ourselves giving every member of the population an enormous number of vitamins and drugs; (2) if people are given vitamins they receive an impression that their diet is defective; (3) the cost to the country is enormous; and (4) people receiving a form of treatment (even if it is prophylactic) are more liable to believe they are unhealthy.

In our attitude to preventive medicine we have got to be careful that too much of the 'can't do harm might do good' argument does not lead to an excess of prevention. We must not be so busy preventing disease that we have no time to enjoy freedom from it.

I read once in an American health pamphlet that every father returning from his day's work should remove his coat and wash his hands in disinfectant before touching any of his children. Perhaps there may be a logical case from the hygienist's point of view, but if that went too far we might finally reach this sort of situation: 'Oh, father, lift me up; there's a band marching past the window'. 'Certainly, my boy; just wait while I gargle and put on my mask and rubber gloves.'

But I must return to my theme, which is that in therapeutics there must be good evidence from controlled statistical trials that what is being given is doing good. Here I should like to issue a warning that the mere use of statistics is no guard against crooked thinking. The danger of crooked statistics is that its fallacies are less likely to be noticed because of the mixture of awe, suspicion, and reverence with which statistical thinking is regarded by most of us.

An Example

Here is an excellent example of statistical crooked thinking. An investigator published an article showing that of 200 epileptic subjects, 24 per cent had had infantile convulsions in the first two years of life, whereas of 200 normal subjects only 2 per cent had had infantile convulsions. He went on to argue that the pronounced difference between the 24 per cent in the epileptics and in the 2 per cent in the control group made it clear that convulsions within the first two years of life ought to be taken as a manifestation of epilepsy and that any child having convulsions in infancy should be treated with anti-convulsant drugs for several years. The argument appears most convincing, doesn't it? The fallacy is not at all obvious. The incidence of epilepsy in the population has been left out. Now, this is about 1 in 400. So among 40,000 people there would be 100 epileptics, 24 of whom had infantile convulsions. But among 40,000 people there would be 800 normal people (2 per cent of 40,000) who had suffered from infantile convulsions. So it would mean treating 800 people, of whom only 24 had epilepsy—in other words, submitting 32 normal children to prolonged anticonvulsant therapy in order to make sure of treating one epileptic early in life. I mention that article in detail to show the danger of being swayed by impressive figures.

CAUSES

Another perversion of thought applicable to statistics is to believe that a statistical relationship between two things implies a causal relationship between them. It does not do so. It is very probable that statistics would show erythroblastosis foetalis to be twenty times less common among the offspring of opium smokers. This is no argument for encouraging opium smoking in the maternity wards. It depends on the fact that opium is largely a Chinese habit and that 99 per cent of Chinese are rhesus-positive, and so cannot produce erythroblastosis foetalis. Similarly, if rheumatic fever is significantly more common in those who have sucked dummy teats in childhood, it may only mean that rheumatic fever is commoner among the poor, and so is dummy-sucking. If A varies with B, it does not show that A causes B.

LOGIC AND THE LABORATORY

I now ask you to consider an attempt at rational thinking applied to the use of laboratory investigations. As regards tests of function, are we not inclined to argue, (1) this test measures the conjugation of benzoic acid; (2) the conjugation of benzoic acid is a function of the liver; (3) therefore this test measures the function of the liver? Might we not equally well argue, (1) this factory produces smoke; (2) this test measures the amount of smoke produced; (3) therefore this test measures the productivity of a factory? The point is that livers and factories both do a number of things, and measuring one of these things does not measure all of them.

Also, it is in the ordering of laboratory or radiological investigations that rational thinking is so necessary. It is a salutary exercise in mental discipline to catechise oneself when ordering any medical investigation, saying, 'Why do I order the test? What am I going to look for in the result? If I find it will it affect my diagnosis? How will this affect my management of the case? Will this ultimately benefit the patient?'

It would be only rarely that we could answer all these questions satisfactorily, as, for instance, in ordering a Wassermann test and a Lange curve on the cerebrospinal fluid of a patient suspected of dementia paralytica. Perhaps it would be a good idea to have a space on every laboratory form in which the doctor had to state exactly why he had ordered a test. I believe if answers were honestly filled in we might get this sort of thing:

(1) I order this test because if it agrees with my opinion I will believe it, and if it does not I shall disbelieve it.

(2) I do not understand this test and am uncertain of the normal figure, but it is the fashion to order it.

(3) When my chief asks if you have done this or that test I like to say, yes, so I order as many tests as I can to avoid being caught out.

(4) I have no clear idea what I am looking for, but in ordering this test I feel in a vague way (like Mr. Micawber) that something might turn up.

(5) I order this test because I want to convince the patient there is nothing wrong, and I don't think he will believe me without a test.

WORDS

Finally, I want to consider the effect of words on thinking. Words not only provide a vehicle for conveying thought, but even provide wings for its flight which make it travel either straight or crooked.

One trouble with words is that if there is a word for a particular thing we become convinced that such a thing exists: this trouble makes precise work so difficult, particularly in the field of psychiatry.

If there is doubt whether, say, a patient is suffering from mania or catatonic schizophrenia, the observer is inclined to think there must be an answer—he believes these two diseases exist as nosological entities. Yet, as there are no truly objective tests to settle the matter, it might be wiser to regard such terms as descriptions of behaviour with no more privilege to exist as diseases in their own right than have conditions such as restlessness, talkativeness, elation, and the like.

It is often helpful to straight thinking to pause and consider what we are meaning by a word, for we may find it is playing tricks on us. Take the word 'typical', for instance. If we hear in a chest those musical rales that may occur in a pneumothorax and we describe them to students as typical, we may convey to the student they are common, whereas we really mean they are classical (always mentioned in books) or diagnostic (making the diagnosis certain).

A similar self-catechism is helpful if we use words like natural, unnatural, normal, or abnormal, or the word 'purpose', and if we ask ourselves exactly what we mean by them we may realise how uncertain we are what we are thinking.

Another source of crooked thinking caused by words arises from the bestowal of a name indicating a pathological process when describing only a symptom or syndrome. We call the common cervico-dorsal myalgia of our out-patients 'fibrositis', but we have no notion whether it is caused by inflammation of fibrous tissue or not. We call the symptoms following gastrectomy 'the dumping syndrome', though there is still no general agreement regarding their cause. Socrates said, 'He who first gave names, gave them according to his conception of the things which they signified, and if his conception was erroneous, shall we not be deceived by him?'

One word which encourages crooked thinking is becoming increasingly popular at the moment—the word 'group'. We say this probably belongs to the allergic group, the psychosomatic group, or the collagen group, without having any very clear idea of the boundaries or contents of those groups. We use them to cloak our ignorance, feeling that once we have cast diseases into these vast receptacles, these aetiological dustbins, they are satisfactorily accounted for. I believe that those brave enough to lift the lids off these bins and poke about among the rubbish there may find clinical salvage of inestimable value.

Another word is to be deplored because it allows woolly thinking to flourish. This is the word 'imbalance'. The word could be expunged from the medical vocabulary without any loss. Whenever we read of autonomic imbalance or endocrine imbalance we are in for a piece of nebulous thinking. It is all right to suggest a disease is associated with overaction of the sympathetic or under-action of the parasympathetic, or due to too much suprarenal cortical secretion or too little thyroid secretion, but to leave it imprecisely labelled as due to imbalance is a travesty of thinking that should not have survived the discipline of a scientific education.

CONCLUSION

I must apologise for the rather vague way I have wandered from one subject to another. All I have tried to suggest is that we ought to be increasingly critical of our own and other people's thinking, to analyse all arguments that our books, our teachers, and ourselves are using; to seek out crooked thinking and avoid it, and to follow the path of straight thinking, wherever it may lead us, guided by those helpers of whom Kipling wrote:

> I keep six honest serving men
> (They taught me all I knew);
> Their names are What and Why and When
> And How and Where and Who.

16

*Munchausen's Syndrome**

Here is described a common syndrome which most doctors have seen, but about which little has been written. Like the famous Baron von Munchausen, the persons affected have always travelled widely; and their stories, like those attributed to him,[1] are both dramatic and untruthful. Accordingly, the syndrome is respectfully dedicated to the baron, and named after him.

The patient showing the syndrome is admitted to hospital with apparent acute illness supported by a plausible and dramatic history. Usually his story is largely made up of falsehoods; he is found to have attended, and deceived, an astounding number of other hospitals; and he nearly always discharges himself against advice, after quarrelling violently with both doctors and nurses. A large number of abdominal scars is particularly characteristic of this condition.

That is a general outline; and few doctors can boast that they have never been hoodwinked by the condition. Often the diagnosis is made by a passing doctor or sister, who, recognising the patient and his performance, exclaims: 'I know that man. We had him in St Quinidine's two years ago and thought he had a perforated ulcer. He's the man who always collapses on buses and tells a story about being an ex-submarine commander who was tortured by the Gestapo.' Equally often, the trickster is first revealed in the hospital dining-room, when, with a burst of laughter, one of the older residents exclaims: 'Good heavens, you haven't got Luella Priskins in again, surely? Why she's been in here three times before and in Barts, Mary's, and Guy's as well. She sometimes comes in with a different name, but always says she's coughed up pints of blood and tells a story about being an ex-opera-singer and helping in the French resistance movement.'

* Published in *The Lancet*, 10th February 1951.

DIAGNOSIS

It is almost impossible to be certain of the diagnosis at first, and it requires a bold casualty officer to refuse admission. Usually, the patient seems seriously ill and is admitted unless someone who has seen him before is there to expose his past. Experienced front-gate porters are often invaluable at doing this.

The following are useful pointers:

1. (Already mentioned) a multiplicity of scars, often abdominal.
2. A mixture of truculence and evasiveness in manner.
3. An immediate history which is always acute and harrowing yet not entirely convincing—overwhelmingly severe abdominal pain of uncertain type, cataclysmal blood-loss unsupported by corresponding pallor, dramatic loss of consciousness, and so forth.
4. A wallet or handbag stuffed with hospital attendance cards, insurance claim forms, and litigious correspondence.

If the patient is not recognised by an old acquaintance, the diagnosis is only gradually revealed by inquiries at other hospitals. Some have given so much trouble elsewhere they have been placed on hospital black-lists. Often the police are found to know the patient and can give many helpful details. Gradually, the true history is pieced together and the patient's own story is seen to be a matrix of fantasy and falsehood, in which fragments of complete truth are surprisingly imbedded. Just as the patient's story is not wholly false, so neither are all the symptoms; and it must be recognised that these patients are often quite ill, although their illness is shrouded by duplicity and distortion. When the whole truth is known, past history sometimes reveals drug-addition, mental-hospital treatment, or prison sentences, but these factors are not constant, and the past may consist solely in innumerable admissions to hospitals and evidence of pathological lying. Often, a real organic lesion from the past has left some genuine physical signs which the patient uses (to quote Pooh Bah) 'to give artistic verisimilitude to an otherwise bald and unconvincing narrative'.

SOME CHARACTERISTIC FEATURES

Most cases resemble organic emergencies. Well-known varieties are:

1. The acute abdominal type (laparotomophilia migrans), which is the most common. Some of these patients have been operated on so often that the development of genuine intestinal obstruction from adhesions may confuse the picture.
2. The haemorrhagic type, who specialise in bleeding from lungs or stomach, or other blood-loss. They are colloquially known as 'haemoptysis merchants' and 'haematemesis merchants'.
3. The neurological type, presenting with paroxysmal headache, loss of consciousness, or peculiar fits.

The most remarkable feature of the syndrome is the apparent senselessness of it. Unlike the malingerer, who may gain a definite end, these patients often seem to gain nothing except the discomfiture of unnecessary investigations or operations. Their initial tolerance to the more brutish hospital measures is remarkable, yet they commonly discharge themselves after a few days with operation wound scarcely healed, or intravenous drips still running.

Another feature is their intense desire to deceive everybody as much as possible. Many of their falsehoods seem to have little point. They lie for the sake of lying. They give false addresses, false names, and false occupations merely from a love of falsehood. Their effrontery is sometimes formidable, and they may appear many times at the same hospital, hoping to meet a new doctor upon whom to practise their deception.

POSSIBLE MOTIVES

Sometimes the motive is never clearly ascertained, but there are indications that one of the following mechanisms may be involved:

1. A desire to be the centre of interest and attention. They may be suffering in fact from the Walter Mitty syndrome,[2] but instead of playing the dramatic part of the surgeon, they submit to the equally dramatic role of the patient.
2. A grudge against doctors and hospitals, which is satisfied by frustrating or deceiving them.
3. A desire for drugs.
4. A desire to escape from the police. (These patients often swallow foreign bodies, interfere with their wounds, or manipulate their thermometers.)
5. A desire to get free board and lodgings for the night, despite the risk of investigations and treatment.

Supplementing these scanty motives, there probably exists some strange twist of personality. Perhaps most cases are hysterics, schizophrenics, masochists, or psychopaths of some kind; but as a group they show such a constant pattern of behaviour that it is worth considering them together.

ILLUSTRATIVE CASE-RECORDS

Three cases of the abdominal type of Munchausen's syndrome are described below; for they show clearly the typical features of the advanced form of the disease. Many other milder forms have been encountered, but it would be tedious if more were described. All the names used in these case-histories have been altered, though most of the names were false to start with; but doctors who have met any of the patients may find that the changed name gives a clue to the original one.

Case 1

A man of 47, giving the name Thomas Beeches, was transferred to the Central Middlesex Mental Observation Ward on May 16 from Harrow Hospital. He had been admitted there on May 13 with suspected intestinal obstruction; laparotomy had shown nothing abnormal. After the operation he had accused the ward sister of tampering with his wallet while he was under the anaesthetic, he had become truculent and demanded his discharge, and because of his violence, and his foolhardiness in wanting to walk out with a day-old laparotomy, he was sent for mental observation.

On examination he was rational and convincing. His abdomen was a mass of scars of various vintage. He explained that while in the Merchant Navy in 1942 he had been torpedoed, suffering multiple abdominal injuries. He was then taken prisoner by the Japanese and kept in in Singapore till 1945. Throughout this time he had multiple discharging faecal fistulae. In 1945, after the liberation of Singapore, he had been taken to Freemantle where he had eleven operations in 7 months (to close the mutiple fistulae), since when he had been continuously at sea till 4 days previously.

The characteristic Munchausen flavour of this history led to further inquiries which revealed that only 8 days previously, while supposed to be at sea, he had been in St James's Hospital, Balham, complaining of acute abdominal pain; and that a year before that he had been in the same hospital and again behaved in the same way. It was further found that in 1943, when he should have been in Singapore, he had been admitted to the Central Middlesex Hospital complaining of 'bursting open of an old torpedo wound' with a discharging sinus in the right iliac fossa. He had then told such a bewildering series of different stories that he had been transferred to Shenley Hospital as a chronic delinquent psychopath, where he was observed for two months and then discharged. At Shenley it was discovered that he had a long history of delinquency and had three past convictions for crime, as well as having been twice in West Park Mental Hospital. (He had escaped both times.) On this present occasion no certifiable abnormality could be found and he was discharged on May 19, three days after admission. No doubt he is still going from one hospital to another.

A fortnight later, a surgical registrar, knowing my interest in Munchausen's syndrome, produced the notes of a case he had encountered at the Norfolk and Norwich Hospital. It was interesting but not surprising to find that it was the same patient. The notes showed that a Thomas Beeches had been admitted on June 23, 1949, as a case of acute intestinal obstruction. He told a story of having been 33 years in the R.A.F. and of having been shot down over Mannheim in 1942, after which he needed 'eight abdominal operations and three short-circuits'. After treatment with morphine, intravenous drip, and gastric suction, he refused a laparotomy and discharged himself against advice on June 26.

Case 2

A woman of 29, giving the name of Margaret Coke, was admitted on June 13, 1948, complaining of three days' severe abdominal pain and vomiting. Her abdomen was a mass of scars. Though admitted from an Edgware address, she gave a home address in Houston, Texas, and said that all her previous operations had been done there, some of them by a 'horse doctor'. Clinically, she appeared to have subacute intestinal obstruction and was treated with morphine and a Miller-Abbot tube; but she discharged herself on June 19 at her own request.

Three weeks later, on July 3, a woman calling herself Elsie Silverborough was admitted to another ward at the Central Middlesex Hospital, having been found collapsed in the street by the police. She gave a home address in Lancashire. It was found she had discharged herself that day from Wembley Hospital, where she had been admitted on the previous day for suspected acute intestinal obstruction. As before, she had been found by the police collapsed in the street. Elsie Silverborough told a story of having had all her previous operations at the Manchester Royal Infirmary, but a surgical registrar recognised her as the Margaret Coke who had been operated on by the Texas horse doctor, and they were proved to be one and the same person.

Inquiries at Manchester Royal Infirmary revealed no trace of either Margaret Coke or Elsie Silverborough having been there, but the day after the identities of these two persons had been merged, a surgical houseman recognised the patient as a certain Elsie Packoma whom he had encountered twice at the Royal Northern Hospital on Oct. 27, 1947, and Nov. 13, 1947. On both occasions she had arrived in casualty smelling of drink and complaining of retention of urine. On the first occasion she was catheterised and then refused all treatment, refused to sign the book or to be admitted, and said she was going to a hotel to call in her private doctor. On the second occasion, she was recognised by the casualty officer and made off before a doctor had seen her. Further inquiries at the Manchester Royal Infirmary revealed that an Elsie Packoma, with a scarred abdomen and a Manchester address, had been admitted as a case of intestinal obstruction on Nov. 15, 1947—two days after discharging herself from the Royal Northern Hospital. No operation had been performed. She had been treated with morphine, Ryle's tube, and enemata, and discharged herself against advice two days after admission.

The triad of Margaret Coke, Elsie Silverborough, and Elsie Packoma was discharged from the Central Middlesex Hospital on July 6, 1948, and nothing further has been heard of it. She told us before she went that she had lived in Piccadilly nearly all her life, working as a prostitute.

Case 3

A woman of 41, giving the name Elsie De Coverley, was admitted to the Central Middlesex Hospital on Feb. 7, 1950, having collapsed on a bus. She gave a history of two days' malaena and one day's severe abdominal pain with vomiting of dark blood. On examination she was apparently in severe pain. Her abdomen was a mass of scars and her veins showed marks of many 'cutting down' operations. Her heart showed a mitral presystolic murmur. She told us that in the last five years she had had two operations for perforation, one for gastro-enterostomy and one for intestinal obstruction, all done at the Royal Devon and Exeter Hospital, where she said she was due to return for a partial gastrectomy.

At first she was diagnosed as a case of a bleeding ulcer with probably a small perforation, but despite her severe pain there was no abdominal rigidity and radiography showed no gas under the diaphragm. Her haemoglobin was 96 per cent and her stools gave only a weakly positive benzidine test. A telephone message to the Royal Devon and Exeter Hospital revealed that she had only once been there in 1944 and had never had an abdominal operation there, but that many other hospitals had made inquiries about her. The patient continued to complain of severe abdominal pain, and a barium meal and gastroscopy had been arranged when she discharged herself against advice on Feb. 15, saying that nobody really thought she had pain.

Since that time an attempt has been made to find out about her past, and here the Royal Devon and Exeter Hospital have been most helpful, because they have been able to trace much of her progress round the country by noting the hospitals that asked after her. More inquiries at these hospitals have each disclosed more admissions at other hospitals, and the complexity of the patient's wanderings grew in the manner of a snowball. I had not the time or the patience to pursue the meanderings completely and the fact that she was found to use nine different names made the project more formidable. The following list of some of her activities is probably incomplete:

In February, 1944, she was admitted to the Royal Devon and Exeter Hospital as Elsie De Coverley from Exeter Prison, with epistaxis.

On April 9, 1947, she was admitted to the Croydon General Hospital as Miss Joan Morris, a shorthand typist, giving a long history of dyspepsia and haematemesis. While being treated with rest and diet she discharged herself two days later.

From Oct. 31 till Nov. 16, 1947, she was in the Royal Sussex Hospital, giving the name Joan Summer, and suspected of having a bleeding leaking ulcer; but at operation the findings were subacute obstruction from adhesions and scarred duodenal ulcer. Gastrojojunostomy was performed. She discharged herself on Nov. 16 against advice, still complaining of severe abdominal pain.

On Dec. 10, 1947, she was admitted to the Croydon General Hospital with acute abdominal pain, 'doubled up in agony', as Mrs

Elsie Layton, a district nurse. She said she was awaiting a partial gastrectomy in Birmingham Hospital. Efforts made to contact her relatives showed that the names and addresses were all false and the patient discharged herself on Dec. 12. She was admitted to Redhill County Hospital a few days after leaving Croydon. She again gave a similar story and discharged herself within a few days.

From Jan. 29 to March 29, 1948, she was in Paddington Hospital, again as Joan Summer, and a laparotomy for bleeding duodenal ulcer was performed; later she complained of severe anginal pain and discharged herself after giving much trouble in the ward.

In March, 1948, she was in the West London Hospital as Joan Lark with alleged pain and bleeding, and discharged herself.

From April 6 to 9, 1948, she was in Fulham Hospital as Joan Summer giving a history of having all her previous operations in York (inquiries at York failed to trace her), and again presenting with alleged abdominal pain and haematemesis. On April 9 she was recognised by a surgeon as Joan Lark of the West London and discharged herself that day.

On July 10, 1948, she was admitted to Guy's Hospital as Joan Malkin, but later said this was an assumed name and gave the name Joan De Coverley, and said all her previous operations had been done at Edinburgh (Edinburgh denied knowing her). At Guy's she was suspected of having a perforated ulcer, but a laparotomy on July 10 showed nothing abnormal except a mass of adhesions, and she discharged herself on July 13, only three days after the operation, and never returned to have her stitches out.

On Jan. 6, 1950, she was admitted to the Royal Free Hospital as Elsie De Coverley, with the usual story. She complained of continuous pain and discharged herself on Jan. 11, saying her sister had just died. (At many hospitals she has given a story of a dying sister.)

On Jan. 18 she was admitted to St Mary Abbots Hospital still as Elsie De Coverley, having collapsed in Kensington High Street with alleged pain and vomiting of blood. On Jan. 20 when told she was not going to have an operation, she pulled out her stomach tube and demanded her immediate discharge.

Later the same day, she was admitted to University College Hospital, and she had a laparotomy on Jan. 25 for suspected perforation. Nothing was found except adhesions. The usual self-discharge followed on Jan. 30.

The same day she was admitted to St Bartholomew's Hospital and discharged herself on Feb. 2.

From Feb. 7 till 15 she was in the Central Middlesex Hospital—see the description at the beginning of this story.

Since leaving us she has remained active, because on March 7 she arrived at the Elizabeth Garrett Anderson Hospital as Jean Hops and was transferred via the Emergency Bed Service to the Royal Free Hospital. The transfer was unfortunate for her because she was recognised by the ward sister and registrar at the Royal Free, where she had been under another name in January this year, and she discharged herself immediately.

On March 27 she was admitted to Middlesex Hospital as Elsie De Coverley, with the usual story of pain and haematemesis, where she remained for three days. She discharged herself when she learnt that inquiries were being made about her at the Royal Devon and Exeter Hospital.

On April 12 she was admitted to the Croydon General, saying she was awaiting a partial gastrectomy at the Royal Devon and Exeter Hospital, and giving a history of severe abdominal pain and bleeding. The Croydon General rang the Royal Devon and Exeter Hospital and while the telephone conversation was being conducted she got out of bed, dressed, and made off.

On April 17 she turned up in Hackney Hospital as Elsie Shackleton, and that is the last that has been heard of her. Probably she is now careful to avoid mentioning the Royal Devon and Exeter Hospital, who have repeatedly exposed her in the past, and, with new names and a slightly different story, is continuing to deceive the few remaining hospitals she has not yet visited.

It seemed worth publishing this rather tedious itinerary in full to show the lengths to which a case of Munchausen's syndrome can develop, and also because it may be a help to surgeons and physicians who are confronted by her case in the future.

CONCLUSION

The syndrome of Baron von Munchausen has been described and three typical cases reported.

These patients waste an enormous amount of time and trouble in hospitals. If any correspondence follows this account, exposing other cases, perhaps some good will have been done. It would be even better if an explanation for the condition could be found, which might lead to a cure of the psychological kink which produces the disease.

REFERENCES

1. Raspe, R. E., *et al.* (1785) *Singular Travels, Campaigns and Adventures of Baron Munchausen*. London: Cresset Press.
2. Thurber, J. (1942) *The Secret Life of Walter Mitty. My World and Welcome To It*. London.